GW01159118

The 2018 Global Migration Compact

Bimal Ghosh

The 2018 Global Migration Compact

A Major Breakthrough or an Opportunity Lost or Both?

Bimal Ghosh
Geneva, Switzerland

ISBN 978-3-030-82862-2 ISBN 978-3-030-82863-9 (eBook)
https://doi.org/10.1007/978-3-030-82863-9

This Palgrave Macmillan imprint is published by the registered company Springer Nature Switzerland AG.
The registered company address is: Gewerbestrasse 11, 6330 Cham, Switzerland

Contents

1

A Global Migration Agreement: Why So Important, Yet Why So Elusive

"Migration is closely interwoven with human history"—the saying sounds like a cliché but it surely remains valid. Time was when cross-border migration was relatively free and unfettered. Military conquests, armed conflicts, famine, pestilence, natural disasters and the like shaped the course of human mobility. Things changed in 1648 when the Westphalia agreement was signed and the concept of sovereignty of nation state was embodied in international law and started gaining ground in state practices. Cross border human mobility became a subject of inter-state negotiation and agreement. And, with the rising trend in economic globalisation, including expansion of trade in goods, services and capital, nation states felt compelled to cooperate in managing cross-border migration to enhance their respective interests, and contribute to global wealth. But not infrequently, the process also entails difficulties.

Experience shows that when cross-border movements are well managed, harmonising the needs and interests of the countries concerned, and ensuring the rights and welfare of the migrants themselves, be it on a bilateral, plurilateral or international basis, this could yield enormous benefits, creating a win-win situation for all parties concerned. It can then be a great opportunity—it can promote growth and increase income,

B. Ghosh, *The 2018 Global Migration Compact*,
https://doi.org/10.1007/978-3-030-82863-9_1

contribute to innovativeness and entrepreneurial initiative and enrich cultural diversity.

If, however migration is badly managed, it could become detrimental to national growth and international development, detrimental to human rights and dignity of migrants, increase social and inter-state tension and can even threaten global peace.

The question then arises: What is specifically meant by "well managed migration"? How does it differ from *badly managed migration*?

Migration can be, and often is, badly managed either in origin or destination (including transit) countries or both. This happens when, for example, migration in origin countries takes place under economic or political *compulsion*, or by a mixture of them and not as a matter of free and rational choice and thus becomes disorderly and disruptive and largely unwanted abroad.

When this happens and receiving countries feel swamped by gathering waves of disruptive and unpredictable inflows and fears grow that immigration is getting out of control, many governments become even more restrictive, creating a vicious circle.

This also happens when, xenophobic prejudice, prevalence of faulty notion, re-enforced by populist propaganda, about the negative consequences of immigration or pressure of vested interest groups, destination countries impose undue restrictions on entry, despite a real demand for migrant workers to meet labour and demographic needs or when migrants are subjected to discrimination and their potential remains un- or under-utilized.

The concurrence of these two happenings makes the situations worse. On the one hand, the origin countries are faced with a rising pressure of disorderly and mostly unwanted emigration, and on the other, the opportunities for legal entry in destination countries keep dwindling.

The challenge for a global migration agreement is to ensure that action is taken at both ends of the flow so that migration becomes regular and that the two conflicting forces—rising emigration pressure in origin countries and dwindling opportunities for legal entry in destination countries—are brought into a dynamic harmony.

The EU, which had earlier followed a "fortress" approach to deal with the pressure of immigration at its external borders, has come to realise the importance of taking action at the end of the origin countries as well, which it has been doing under the labels of "global approach" (see Chap. 3) and more recently, "partnership agreements". The destination countries openness should not be unfettered, but regulated in keeping with an agreed set of norms and principles reflecting the needs and conditions of both groups of countries.[1]

As for the origin countries, it is useful to make a distinction between survival migration and opportunity-seeking migration Briefly speaking, survival migrants move under the compulsion of poverty, hunger, despair or political persecution. They move not out of their own volition, but because they are forced to do so. They are apt to feel they have little to lose by taking the risk of seeking to move through any available irregular channel. By contrast, for opportunity-seeking migrants the movement is a matter of choice, based on a rational assessment of the costs and benefits involved. They are also more likely to have an adequate knowledge of the basic conditions in the destination countries. Also, unlike irregular migrants they prepare themselves well in advance, and would normally avoid the costs and risks of irregular entry (Ghosh 1998a, b).

Under a well-managed migration system, origin countries would be open to opportunity-seeking migration, and try to avoid or at least minimise survival migration by attacking the root causes.

1.1 Global Migration: Gains from Well-Managed Migration

Countries differ in the supply of labour relative to the availability of capital and other resources or endowments. So, labour mobility from a labour-surplus country, suffering from high unemployment to a labour-short and capital-rich country yields all-round benefits. It leads to a more efficient use of labour and narrows inter-country wage differences. The origin countries benefit from less unemployment and a boost for

[1] For a discussion on the superiority of regulated openness over unfettered open borders see Bimal Ghosh, "Managing Migration: Towards the Missing Regime" *in Migration without Borders,* UNESCO, Paris 2008.

economic growth through remittances and access to strategic inputs and improved skills in case of return. The receiving country gains as immigration removes labour scarcity, facilitates occupational mobility and often leads to a country's human capital stock. By doing so, it reduces wage-push inflationary pressure, helps fuller utilisation of productive capital, and thus boosts economic growth. The migrants themselves gain from higher wages and improved productivity in the destination country.

But labour is not a unitary commodity; its efficacy often varies between countries, depending on the levels of workers' education, their sector/industry-specific skills and aptitude, technology used and other factors. In estimating the real benefits, account must also be taken of the aggregate labour efficacy of the migrant.

The availability and levels of specific skills also matter. Even a country with a low general level of labour efficiency may be rich in certain specific skills. An exchange of such skills through migration also yields reciprocal benefits for them. (further discussed in Chap. 2).

Already in 1984, an estimate made Hamilton and Whaley showed that the efficiency from removal of barriers to labour mobility across countries could double the global income. Another estimate made in 2004, shows that even a 10% increase in international labour mobility would generate an annual economic gain, adjusted for inter-country differences in labour efficiency, of about $774 billion income gain in 1998 dollar (Moses et al. 2004) Similarly, a recent analysis by Dan Rodrik at Kennedy School of Government showed that since wages for similarly qualified workers in developed and developing countries differ sharply—by a factor of 10 or more as against a difference for commodities and financial assets that rarely exceed a ratio of 1:2, the gains from labour mobility could be enormous—roughly 25 times larger than the gains from liberalisation of movement of capital and goods (Rodrik 2002). He also estimated that even a modest increase in temporary admission of poor country workers of no more than 3 percent of rich countries' labour force could yield a benefit of $200 billion for the developing world.

To illustrate further, a recent IMF study shows that a 1 (one) per cent increase in share of adult population of a receiving country increases GDP per person by 2% in the long term (Jaumotte et al. 2016). Likewise, in 2005 the World Bank estimated that a rise in emigration from developing countries equal to 3% of the labour force of high-income countries could lead to an output gain of US $356 billion by 2025, of which the developing countries would have US$ 143 billion and their migrants US$162 billion, adjusted for differences in purchasing power between high income and developing countries (World Bank 2005). Migrants represent 3.4% of the world population but contribute 10% of the global income, and 85% of the migrants' earnings are spent in host countries, enriching their economies.

Most of these macro-economic estimates are of course incomplete in the sense that they do not take full account of all the negative externalities, including the human and social costs, of cross-border movements. These models are based on a set of fixed assumptions which are not always valid. Aside from the question of differences in efficacy of labour, it assumes that perfect competition and mobility exist in labour markets; that there are no public goods or no public intervention and that both economies of scale in production and output mix in the economies remain unchanged (see also Clemens 2011). The reality is often different. They are nonetheless indicative of enormous economic benefits that the world can reap from safe and orderly migration.

These income benefits for the world economy become clearer if analysed in three specific areas.: labour market, public finance and technological change, in the country- or region-specific situations, as briefly done below.

1.2 Labour Markets

Well-manged migration can help meet the shortage and gaps in the receiving countries labour force and enhance economic growth. Between 2004 and 2014 immigrants accounted for 47% of the increase in the workforce in the USA and 70 percent in Europe (OECD 2014) just as they accounted for 31% increase in the highly educated labour force in Canada, 21% in the USA and 14% in Europe. Recent immigrants, especially, the younger ones, have significantly contributed to the increase in highly educated labour force in these countries. Between 2000/2001 and

2014 immigrants contributed 31% to the increase in the highly educated work force in Canada, 21% in the USA and 14% in Europe.

Immigrants can also meet labour market gaps and imbalances. They have been doing this in the dynamic sectors of the economy such as health care occupations and those in science, technology and engineering sectors. At the same time immigrants are filling in labour needs in a number of declining occupations, representing about a quarter of entries (24%) in Europe and 28% in the USA. In all these occupations immigrants are taking up jobs regarded by domestic workers as unattractive or lacking career prospects. This shows the how migrants can provide a mix of skills across the economy as an essential requirement for growth. (further discussed below).

The OECD has estimated that free movement of people has lowered average unemployment across Europe by 6%; another OECD study covering a 25-year period (1980–2005) showed that increased migration is co-related to commensurate increases to total employment and growth. Likewise, the EU Commission found that between 2004 and 2006 migration from eight new member states had lowered average unemployment of old EU member states by 6%. It also found that immigrants within the EU had boosted the region's aggregate growth by 0.28% since 2004.

1.3 Innovation and Technological Change

Migration can also be an important source of innovation and entrepreneurial spirit and contribute to creation of jobs and income, and do not necessarily take away jobs from domestic workers or depress their wages. Companies in most industrial countries have enormously benefited from skilled migrant inflows. In the USA two-thirds of Silicon Valley companies were started by people of foreign origin. Cypress Semiconductor Corporation recently reported that about 40% of research and development jobs were held by skilled migrants and that each job created nine additional jobs (Migration News,1997, Ghosh 2010).

Evidence abounds. A study by William Kerr of Harvard Business School revealed that nearly 40% of patents by Intel, a chip-maker, were for work done by people of Chinese or Indian origin. Another study in

2008 by William Kerr and William Lincoln showed interchange of ideas also helped the US-born scientists. This is also illustrated by the fact that when the government increased the number of (skilled) H1-B entrants by 10% total patents increased by 2%. At the same, skilled migration need not necessarily be a permanent loss for the origin countries. This can be avoided when ethnic networking leads scientists and technicians at home to establish close contacts with those who have the same national origin but now living and working abroad in a technologically advanced country and tap their skills, talents and other resources, as it seems to be happening with Indian scientists and its diaspora counterparts in the USA (Agarwal et al. 2008).

Most recently, the Pfizer/BioNTech covid-19 vaccine, an amazing scientific achievement, was developed by people of migrant origin—the outcome of close collaboration between Turkish-German scientists, with external support for production.

The above should not overshadow an interesting point about skill composition of the labour force of a country. An essential condition of growth is the availability of a mix of skills across occupations and sectors; this includes low-level sills. (further discussed below).

1.4 Public Finance

A study by Liebig and Mo in 2013 examines the cumulative fiscal impact of immigration in all European OECD countries as well as Australia, Canada and the USA over the past 50 years (OECD 2014). It shows that the net fiscal effect of immigration in OECD countries is *on average* nearly zero, rarely exceeding 0.5% in either positive or negative terms. There are however exceptions: in Switzerland and Luxenberg immigrants contribute a net benefit of about 2% of GDP to the public exchequer.

Calculations for Germany by Bonnin and others (2000) showed that an annual immigration flow of 0.25% of the resident population can reduce by 30% the tax burden of future-born Germans if aggregate net payments made by immigrants were evenly distributed among them. According to the country's employment agency, Sweden needs an inflow of 64,000 immigrants per year to avoid labour shortage and sustain its social welfare system, assuming that all these foreigners will have the same rate of employment as Swedish workers, (which however is unlikely).[2]

Contrary to the popular perception, migrants contribute more in taxes and social contributions than they receive in individual benefits.

1.5 Downside of Poorly Managed Migration

When migration is badly managed, not only are these enormous potential gains and opportunities foregone, but it also leads to a string of perverse results, causing economic costs, human sufferings and social perils. As I have argued elsewhere, when there is a high, real demand for immigrants to meet labour shortages and demographic decline in potential destination countries and high emigration pressure due to poverty, unemployment or persecution in origin countries, and especially when the two coincide, unilateral restrictions at either end do not stop migration, it drives migration into irregular channels, as has often happened over the years, with all its associated ills.

Governments have been spending enormous amounts of taxpayers' money on border control and construction of high walls and high-tech fences to enforce mostly unitarily imposed restrictive policies and stop irregular entries. A recent estimate shows that between 2000 and 2015 the EU governments spent EUR 13 billion on border control, including costly evictions and sending back irregular migrants, while migrants themselves paid EUR 16 billion to traffickers to enter Europe (Migrant Files 2015).

In the USA, former president, Donald Trump had called for US$ 18 billion over 10 years for constructing and fortifying the US/Mexico, border wall and the actual cost was ballooning (the new administration cancelled the project). The USA had already doubled its border control personnel over the past decade and its parent agency, Customs and Border Protection, had seen its budget of US$ 5.9 billion in 1954 to more than

[2] This is unlikely to be the case. Experience shows in Sweden foreigners are 2.6 times more likely to be out of work.

US$12 billion in 2014 and may have spent US$20 billion during the period. The INS (Immigration and Naturalization Service) budget, roughly half of which was devoted to enforcement, including preventing irregular immigration, rose 20-fold from US$250 million in 1980 to about US$ 5 billion in 2000.

In the same period, the estimated number of irregular migrants rose from 3 million to 9 million in spite of a number of regularisation programmes (IOM,2005). Since then, defying all the expensive and elaborate measures, irregular migration has continued. An estimated 11.3 million irregular migrants were living in the USA in 2016 (Krogstad et al. 2017). A large number of irregular migrants, estimated to be between 1.9 million and 3.8 million, was living in EU-27 in 2008 (Kovacheva and Vogel 2009). An estimate made around the same time showed the irregular migration represented between one-third or more of the yearly legal migration in the USA and half in Europe (Ghosh 1998a, b). Since then there seems to have been a slight decline in irregular migration flows, but it continues to fluctuate, depending, *inter alia*, on the global economic cycle and immigration policies of the potential destination countries.

In these countries during a phase of economic down-turn many firms, especially in declining industries, actively search for cheap and docile irregular migrant workers to survive. When their economies are in an upward economic swing, and they have unmet labour demand, restrictive labour immigration policies drive labour immigration through irregular channels.

As the faulty, unilaterally imposed restrictive policies encourage irregular, disorderly and mostly unwanted immigration, the risks of human rights violations also rise. The desperate migrants trying to flee persecution, deprivation or extreme poverty are not just financially fleeced by ruthless traffickers.

Human trafficking, increasingly interlocked with trafficking in drugs, and arms and as well as with prostitution of women and child abuse, was rising, with anything between 10 and 12 billion US dollars according to an estimate in 2005. The United Nations Office on Drugs and Crimes, estimates that in 2018 as many as about 50,000 trafficking victims were detected and reported by 148 countries. The share of boys increased five times in the past 15 years while that of children had tripled. It also warned that COVID-induced recession was likely to expose more people to the risk of trafficking.

The desperate migrants trying to flee persecution, deprivation or extreme poverty are not just financially fleeced by ruthless traffickers but are physically abused. and not infrequently pay the ultimate price with life—since 1994 over 18,500 migrants have been recorded dead or missing on their way to Europe on the Mediterranean route alone, prompting Pope Francis to call it a "cemetery". More than 33,400 migrants—men, women and children—died or were reported missing globally since 2014.

A well-designed global migration agreement, laying down common norms and principles among nations, can help ensure achieving a system of migration, capable of yielding the benefits of cross border movements, while avoiding the negative consequences of poorly managed migration, as mentioned above. It can help reduce the pressure for irregular, unsafe and disruptive emigration in origin countries and help open up opportunities for regular and more predictable entries in destination countries, without causing them fearful of losing control over their borders. Also, it can ensure protection of migrants' rights and their fair treatment at both ends of the flow.

The pre-existence of such a global framework will also help in confidence building among all states. It will give destination countries more confidence in the migration system and feel more inclined to respect rules concerning the rights and welfare of migrants on their territories. It will also give confidence to the weaker ones, and facilitate free and fair negotiations at regional and bilateral levels. It will make easier for regional groupings like the EU to manage external migration and ensure smooth operation of the system of free internal movement.

1.6 Polarisation of the Migration Debate

It is however important to note that even when countries as a whole gain from well-managed migration, it often affects different groups differently both within and between origin and destination countries. This presents a real difficulty in reaching an agreement on migration even at the national level and becomes part of national politics, and alongside national politics, the debate on migration becomes increasingly polarized.

Extremist conservative parties and other anti-migration groups paint migration only as an unmixed negative phenomenon, harmful for the integrity and economy of a nation and a threat to the control of its borders. This is reflected in ex-US president Trump's promise to build a wall along its Mexican border and the Brexit movement in Britain to "take back control of borders "from the European Union".

The right-winged populist movement, holding unmixed negative views of immigration has been gaining ground in many countries. (see Table 1.1). Indicative of the trend are the fears of immigration whipped up by Victor Urban in Hungary, just as it is reflected in the anti-immigration policy trends of the Freedom Party in Austria, the League in Italy and the rising popularity of the National Front, now baptized as National Rally (Réassemblèment National) in France, and Sweden Democrats in Sweden. Some of the slogans used are startling as they say

Table 1.1 Increase in the right-wing political parties share in votes

Country	Party and percentage	
1. Hungary	Fidesz 49%	Jobbik 19.6%
2. Austria	Freedom party 26%	
3. Switzerland	Swiss freedom party 25.8%	
4. Denmark	Danish People's party 21%	
5. Belgium	New Flemish Alliance 20.4%	
6. Estonia	Conservative People's party 17.8%	
7. Finland	The Finns 17.7%	
8. Sweden	Sweden democrats 17.6%	
9. Italy	The league 17.4%	
10. Spain	Vox 15%	
11. France	National rally 13%	
12. Netherlands	Freedom party 13%	
13. Germany	Alternative for Germany 12.6%	
14. Czech Republic	Freedom and democracy party 11%	
15. Bulgaria	United patriots 9%	
16. Slovakia	Our Slovakia 8%	
17. Poland	Confederation 6.8%	
18. Greece	Greek solution 3.7%	
19. Cyprus	Elam 3.7%	

Source: BBC

or imply that immigration is a threat to western civilization, which badly needs to be saved from the peril.

As a reaction to these negative policies and propaganda, the pro-migration entities go to the other extreme. In framing their rebuttal these entities, including some UN agencies, tend to profile migration as an unmixed blessing. While narrating the positive effects of migration, they forget to speak of the direct and indirect costs of migration, and ignore to mention the negative consequences of badly managed migration or make just a passing reference to it. Lately, however, some of them have started becoming alive to the shortcomings of this lop-sided trend in the current discourse on migration. To illustrate, Antonio Vitorino, director general of the International Organization for Migration, recently admitted that the social discourse on migration is too often framed in binary terms: those in favour of migration and those against it.

It is almost like a shouting match between two opposing groups in which the sane voice of a thoughtful balance has no place. When the states, gripped by extremism, are so sharply divided internally on migration, it is clearly more difficult for them to reach an agreement at the global level, as revealed by the long history of past attempts at reaching it (see Chap. 3).

Aside from these overarching constraints, some analysts believe that a number of specific difficulties stand in the way of achieving a sustainable global agreement or regime on migration. How real are these difficulties? This is discussed in the next chapter.

References

Agarwal A., D. Kapur, and J. McHale. 2008. Brain Drain or Brain Bank? The Impact of Skilled Emigration on Poor-country Innovation. NBER Working Paper 1459w2Mooe *2008,* Brian Drain or Bran Bank.

Clemens, M.A. 2011. Economics and emigration: Trillion-dollar bills on the sidewalk. *Journal of Economic Perspectives* 25 (3): 83–106.

Ghosh, B. 1998a. Tame Europe's black economy in *International Herald Tribune*, 10 June 1998.

———. 1998b. *Huddled masses and uncertain shores: Insight into irregular migration*. The Hague: Martinus Nijhoff Publishers/Kluwer Law International.
Jaumotte, Florence et al. 2016. Impact of migration on income levels in advanced economies. IMF e Library, October 2016.
Krogstad, Passel and Cohen, 2017. Migration Data Portal 9 June 2020.
Kovacheva and Vogel, 2009. Migration Data Portal 9 June 2020.
Moses, Jonathan, et al. 2004. The economic costs to international labour restrictions: Revisiting the empirical discussion. In *World development*. World Bank.
OECD "Is Migration Good for the Economy" Migration Policy Debate 2014. Paris.
Rodrik, D. 2002. Feasible globalizations. In *Globalization: What's new?* ed. M. Weinstein, 96–213. New York: Colombia University Press. Also, working paper series RWP02029, pp.19–20.
World Bank. "The Potential Gains from Migration" 2005. Washington DC.

2

Multilateral Migration Agreement and Perceived Obstacles: How Valid Are They?

Three specific reasons are generally cited for holding up the development of a regime of inter-state cooperation on migration and sustain it:

(a) lack of a shared interest or a "common good" (defined as those facilities, material or otherwise, that the members of a community provide to all members in order to fulfil a reciprocal obligation for certain interests that they have in common.)
(b) asymmetric interest and bargaining power of countries of origin and destination and.
(c) absence of a hegemonic power to sponsor and safeguard such a regime.

Additionally, some are opposed to a global agreement on the theoretical argument that the state has the prerogative of controlling its borders, it will be an abdication of its authority if outsiders are allowed to interfere in its management.

All these perceived constraints relate to a comprehensive migration agreement. However, as concerns specific migrant groups or aspects of migration, nations had already been able to reach agreements as reflected in, for example, a series of ILO and UN instruments on migrants' human

B. Ghosh, *The 2018 Global Migration Compact*,
https://doi.org/10.1007/978-3-030-82863-9_2

and labour rights. Even on the issue of freedom of movement, there are international instruments for specific groups of potential migrants and special migratory situations such as the rights of a child to move to a country where the child's best interest lies; the right to seek asylum in a foreign country by persons under individual political persecution and the right of a national to return to his or her own country.

None of these international agreements deals with the whole ambit of migration and in a cohesive manner, needed to make global migration more orderly, safe and regular. Also, the international community has generally found it easier to build a consensus for collective, punitive and preventive action against criminal and grossly dehumanising activities than for promotional and pro-active measures. The speed with which the international community moved to adopt in 2000 international instruments against human trafficking and migrant smuggling is indicative of this trend.

But developing a global consensus on migration management in a comprehensive and cohesive manner, involving multiple stakeholders with a variety of both converging and conflicting interests and concerns, is quite a different matter. The difficulties and misgivings implicit in the process are manifold, making the negotiation complex, though much of the perceived constraints to its fruition is of doubtful validity. This is discussed below.

2.1 Lack of Shared Interest

All civilised states have a collective as well as individual stake in maintaining international stability and peace and promoting economic progress. The importance of this stake is heightened by planetary problems and perils such as those related to the deteriorating environment, and pandemics like COVID. It is also unveiled by the new opportunities arising out of inter-penetrations of markets and economies and inter-dependence of nations. Orderliness and predictability in human mobility are among the essential conditions of achieving these goals of peace, stability and economic progress and these thus constitute the "common good" (defined as facilities—material or otherwise—that members of a community provide to all members in order to fulfil a relational obligation they all have to care for certain interests that they have in common) to underpin a global agreement on migration, fully in keeping with the tenets of traditional regime theories.

There is also the human rights argument in favour of inter-state cooperation to manage migration. Protection of human rights and good management of migration are closely related, and the nexus makes a compelling case for states to cooperate for the sake of both (Ghosh 2003). Under international human rights law, states have an obligation to protect human rights of all those within its territory and jurisdiction. And, as Guy Goodwin-Gill puts it, protection of migrants extends even into the areas of sovereign competence (Goodwin-Gill 2000). He argues that given the manifestly international dimension of migratory and refugee movements, there is a collective duty of states to protect the persons moving across borders. It is therefore incumbent upon them to cooperate and achieve this goal. These human rights obligations are, he further points out, also embedded in the cooperative framework established by the United Nations Charter and general international law.[1]

2.2 Asymmetric Interest and Bargaining Power

As concerns the issue of asymmetric bargaining power, the argument has remained opaque. It can be seen as an issue of supply-demand disequilibrium—more candidates for emigration than the number of entry slots available at the receiving end. However, with the (slowly) rising trends towards the creation of free movement zones (and mobility both within and between zones)—and increase, however modest, of arrangements for dual nationality, this argument loses some of its strength.

Another facet, related to this line of argument, may allude to the unequal interest and lack of reciprocity between origin and destination

[1] Article 1(3) of the United Nations Charter, for example, specifies the duty of states to cooperate "in solving international problems of an economic, social, cultural and human character, and in promoting and encouraging respect for human rights ..."

countries. Destination countries, it is argued, can have easy access to expectant emigrants who are abundant in supply. By contrast, origin counties, which are anxious to let them go, and are willing to comply with rich countries' demand, have no corresponding leverage vis-à-vis the destination countries. There is therefore no reciprocity allowing a trade-off between the two groups.

The notion underlying the argument may also refer to the weaker economic and political power of the origin (or sending) countries in the global South vis-à-vis the destination (or receiving) countries in the industrial North. If so, this is not borne out by facts revealing the direction of recent migratory flows.

True, there is some historical evidence that in the past much of international migration, especially major flows, had been from poor and weak countries to rich and powerful countries. The former provided the "push" and the latter the 'pull' as drivers of migration. Several theories, too, had flourished to explain the situation. These included: conflict or centre-periphery theory and its two variants: dual market theory and world systems theory, both emphasising the exploitation of poor countries' cheap labour to feed the permanent demand of industrialised countries, while inhibiting the growth of manufacturing industries in poor countries themselves. The simple message emanating from these theories is: migration is good for rich countries but bad for the poor ones.

There may have been an element of validity in these theories during the period of colonialism. But, as in trade, modern migration is driven mainly by comparative advantages, associated with specialisation, enjoyed by different countries. Even a poor and weak country may have niches of strength because of its tradition and specialisation in some specific crafts and labour-intensive industries or services. It is the changing diversity in comparative advantages enjoyed by the countries and complementing each other's needs that shapes the direction of much of modern labour migration flows.

Although the concept of comparative advantage applies primarily to labour migration, this has relevance to other types as well. For instance, a country may be economically poor, but it may have a comparative advantage in climatic conditions and nursing services. These may make it a destination country for health-related migration.

Increasingly, global migration is taking place both within and between the groups of rich and the poor countries. This reality is reflected in the changing directions of the global migration flows in recent years and reveals the deficiency of the argument that all origin countries suffer from lower bargaining power.

Already in 2010, South-South migration reached 18.5 million as against the South-North migration flow of 21.7 million, and North-North migration of 9 million. The underlying trend saw further momentum in the following years. Thus by 2015, the South-South migration (90.2 million) surpassed South-North migration (85.3 million), while North-North migration flow also rose to 13.7 million. There was also North-South migration of 13.7 million. The changing directions and configuration of global migration flows are indicative of the economic diversity and related comparative advantages of different countries.

It will be wrong, therefore, to suggest that global migration is always a one-way flow—from poor and weak countries to rich and powerful countries.

The fact that, as narrated above, all civilised states have certain common stakes and interests does not deny the reality that the individual states also have differing, even conflicting, interests on many individual issues, depending on the country-specific situation. But it is precisely this diversity in state interests that offers huge potential of bargaining based on trade-offs or reciprocity, as practised in trade negotiation, making each country a net gainer at the of the deal.

This apart, even assuming that all origin countries are poor and weak, and all destination countries are rich and powerful, there is quite a large number of potential areas of reciprocity of interests between them that can be explored within the framework of a general migration agreement.

These areas include: trade-off between opportunities for legal entry in destination countries and return/readmission of irregular migrants to countries of origin; availability of negotiated categories of skilled workers to origin countries in exchange of predictable supply of the origin countries' less-skilled workers in response to meet the destination countries' labour needs in seasonal industries and occupations, and unmet labour demand in industries and services, generally shunned by locals.

Some scope also exists for negotiating reciprocity between movements of rich countries' high-level personnel as intra-company transfers under mode 3 (commercial presence of the General Agreement on Trade in Services) and temporary entry into advanced economy countries of developing countries' service-providing professionals both as employees and as self-employed persons. Significant trade-offs may also be explored between predictable labour supply from origin countries and alleviation of the growing strain on social security funding and the demographic decline in (industrial) destination countries.

Reciprocity of interests *across sectors*—for example, access of migrants to destination countries' labour markets in exchange for liberalisation of origin countries' specific product markets as was discussed during the Doha round of international trade negotiation—also holds some significant promise. To illustrate, origin countries may agree to liberalise their agricultural commodities market, if in exchange the destination countries agree to accept some additional labour migrants from origin countries, as was discussed during these talks. India offered freer access for rich countries' specific products to its markets if such countries accepted some additional Indian labour migrants.

Although the principle of reciprocity of interests has underpinned some of the existing bilateral agreements, they have been generally confined to certain specific issues. Outside the European Union, formal reciprocal commitments have generally been limited to issues like readmission, remittances and planned recruitment, all within the realm of migration, and mostly in a bilateral context. Unlike in the case of trade, neither individual governments nor international organisations have explored the full range of reciprocity that can be negotiated within the migration area itself or across sectors.

When fair treatment of a country's emigrants and immigrants becomes intertwined, cementing the reciprocity of the two groups of countries.

An overarching rebuttal of the argument of lack of shared interests lies in the erosion of the dichotomy between sending and receiving countries as more and more countries are becoming involved in both sending and receiving migrants at the same time. According to a recent global survey by the ILO, at least 25% of states are both major senders and major receivers of migrants. (ILO 1999).[2]

They are therefore required to ensure the protection and fair treatment of the immigrants on their territory just as they would like to see this done for their own migrants abroad (the nation state has a basic obligation to ensure the human rights and fair treatment including safety and welfare of their nationals even when they are abroad, as already discussed, (page 17). A global agreement is the surest means of ensuring adherence to this balanced and equitable two-way approach to migration management and avoiding *tit-for-tat* state practices. Although often ignored, or forgotten, it shows how the protection of migrants' human rights and good governance of migration are closely interwoven.

As for the role of a hegemonic power in regime formation, the situation has significantly evolved over time, signalling a diminishing global influence of one or more hegemonic powers alongside the rising emergence of a multi-polar world society, buoyed by widely dispersed soft power and inter-dependence of nations Not surprisingly, in recent years several international agreements or regimes were initiated and/or subsequently sustained by collective initiatives in the United Nations, despite the absence of any hegemonic support or even resistance from one or more hegemonic states. In these cases, collective consensus-building rather than hegemonic leadership was the driving force.

It is worth recalling that although the USA and Germany were in the forefront of the 2016 Global Compact initiative, they first sought to build a collective consensus of nations in its favour, which found expression in the New York Declaration, and paved the way for the adoption of the Compact. (see Chap. 4 below).

[2] ILO, Migrant Workers, 1999, Geneva. 'major is defined as including only countries whose labour market or gnp was affected to an extent of at least 1% by international labour migrants, disregarding asylum-seekers and refugees'.

Is Sovereignty an Obstacle to an Inter-State Agreement on Global Migration?

Basic to the concept of sovereignty is a state's prerogative to protect its borders and to decide who may or may not enter its territory. If nation states cooperate closely in managing migration, does it imply that they are abdicating an integral part of this authority? Some seem to think that any such cooperation is indeed an intrusion into state sovereignty or at least a dilution of its authority in a domain which is strictly its own. So, an inter-state agreement on migration is indeed incompatible with state sovereignty.

The idea is however seriously flawed. It seems to be based on an inadequate understanding of the historical evolution of the nation state and of the basic nature and characteristics of inter-state cooperation needed for collectively managed migration.

The concept of state sovereignty as it emerged out of the Westphalia conference in 1648 should not be seen as a static one. History shows modern states have been accustomed to developing new forms and areas of cooperation in response to new and evolving needs and conditions in the world. But for such cooperation, shared values and agreed norms of conduct, the very survival of nation-states might have been at stake. These norms provide the basis of inter-state relations and much of the sources of international law in a civilised world society.

The interpenetration of markets and economies, the growth of transnational communities, including systems of dual nationalities and emerging concepts of post-national human rights and citizenship, are no doubt having a discernible impact on the traditional authority and behaviour of the nation state, with a shift of attention, especially since the end of the Cold War, towards inter-state cooperation and coalition. Environmental issues, including natural disasters, and pandemics and spread of infectious diseases, have lent urgency and importance to such joint action to deal with transnational or extra-territorial issues. Migration is one such issues.

Admittedly, international migration differs from other forms of exchanges or types of cross-border movements such as flow of goods and capital in one particularly important respect: it involves people, and not inanimate objects. This makes it more sensitive *vis-à-vis* territorial sovereignty, which nation states seek to zealously protect and preserve. But this also makes the stakes in the whole game of managing migration particularly high. It is precisely this human aspect that makes the perils of mismanaging migration particularly alarming, thus highlighting the imperative need of its better management through new forms of global cooperation.

The model of inter-stater cooperation implicit in an agreement for better management of migration should not be confused with a supranational construct or seen as an externally imposed constraint on the nation state. It is a freely negotiated arrangement of convenience between and among nation states, which Germany's ex-chancellor, Helmut Kohl had once called 'pooling of national sovereignties,' enhances and enriches nation states' capacity to deal with extra- or supra-territorial aspects of international migration. It is also an expression of the continuing evolution of the nation state, and not of a diminished concern for its territorial integrity or of an erosion of its sovereignty.

2.3 Migration Agreement: Global or Regional?

Some analysts, though supportive of a plurilateral migration agreement, would prefer to have it designed on a regional rather than global basis. The two main arguments in favour of a regional approach are: (a) much of cross border movements are intra-regional rather than inter-regional and (b) confidence building is easier—or rather less difficult—to reach an agreement on a regional level than on a global level. Underlying both these arguments is the assumption that geographic proximity provides a vantage point for initiating regional policy coordination as the countries within a specific region are more likely to have a shared interest and a common concern to manage migration through joint action.

There is also a practical consideration favouring a regional approach. Several powerful industrial countries had in the past been averse to becoming engaged in what they perceived to be a long-drawn out process of negotiation on a sensitive subject like cooperative management of global migration. These governments seemed to think the challenge was too complex and too overwhelming to be tackled at the global level. Some of them—which were willing to explore new ways of promoting co-operation in managing migration—felt more comfortable to do so in a regional context. Some others that perceived migration more as a "problem" and wanted to "contain" it within the confines of the region producing the flow, "beyond the developed world". This then serves as an extension of the "policy of containment" as part of now outdated isolationist statecraft.

Indeed, a regional approach does have some attractive features and it is reflected in a (modestly) increasing number of free-movement regions and sub-regions, (although in many cases they still remain to be fully operational). But it also suffers from several pitfalls and deficiencies in ensuring a sound management of migration. And even if some of the arguments favouring a regional approach have a degree of validity, the limitations of an exclusively global approach are also clear, as discussed below.

First, as concerns the predominance of intra-regional movements, it is true, a large proportion of migration takes place within the same region, but the pattern is neither constant nor uniform. Barring a few exceptions, the main sources of migration and destination countries are not necessarily located in the same region. To illustrate, contrary to the popular impression, a high proportion of the inflows to the US and the EU stem from outside the respective regions. In Europe, for example, figures for recent years showed that almost half of the foreign population resident in industrial (northern and western) Europe was from outside the European region, and the trend seems to have continued. For example, in 1997, immigration into the EU from outside Europe accounted for around 41% of the total flow. If Eastern Europe were excluded, and considered as a separate region, the percentage would be as high as 55%.[3]

[3] Past figures for most individual EU countries showed a similar trend. In 2002 , the share of the non-EU nationals in the total number of immigrants 71% in Italy, 66% in Austria, 57% in Germany, 56% in Sweden and 52% in the Netherlands, (Eurostat 2002: 11)

In the case of the United States, the number of admissions of permanent immigrants from Asia accounted for an average 47.7 of admissions from all regions in 1980–84 and 41.8% in 1990–94, compared with 41.5% and 36.7%, respectively, from the American region, including Canada.

Also, the activities of traffickers, who are extremely agile in changing their routes across regions in response to their tactical needs, suggest the importance of a global approach. This is reflected in the global approach and scope of the UN instrument against transnational organised crime and its two more recent protocols.

It is not just that the main source, transit and destination countries are not always located in the same region. More importantly, in an increasingly globalized world when there are changes in the surrounding circumstances, including policy changes, the direction of the flows tends to change quickly. For example, tightening of immigration control in one region (e.g., western Europe) is likely to add to pressures for immigration in other region (e.g., North America) or regions and *vice versa*. As a consequence, the directional pattern of the flows may change quickly.

Geographic Proximity and Confidence-Building

Second, confidence building is supposed to be easier and negotiation less onerous within a small group of contiguous countries, especially when there is a high degree of economic and social convergence, as in the case of the EU. This provides a vantage point for initiating regional policy coordination as the countries within a specific region are more likely to have a shared interest and a common concern to manage migration through joint action.

In reality, however, confidence building within a contiguous region may prove to be more, rather than less, difficult within a specific region, especially if it is marked by glaring economic and political disparities. Experience shows that fear and mistrust of powerful neighbouring countries, holding hegemonic influence, may create tension and may hold up genuine cooperation even in times of crises. And even the EU, with a degree of its intra-regional equality, suffers from this difficulty. Periodic tensions between the southern European countries and those in the north-west over burden-sharing related to external migration, budgetary issues and the like are well known. The same applies to cooperation between western Europe and central/eastern Europe. Even Germany's predominance among "equals" within the EU states has occasionally created internal tension and heated arguments, some of which has found public expressions.

The history of the North-South dialogue in the 1970s', the emergence of the Group of 77 and its efforts to develop economic and technical cooperation (ECDC) across regions show that economically less affluent, politically less powerful countries are often fearful of the more dominant states and the leverage they enjoy in any regional negotiation. They feel less fearful and more comfortable in a global setting, marked by the diversity or mix of countries and diffused hegemonic influence.

This is true also of striking inequality within developing regions. As a few years ago the United Nations report of an international conference noted, regional cooperation in southern Arica on management of international migration "had its limitations due to enormous differentials between countries such as 40-fold gap in income between South Africa and Mozambique." (UNICEF 1998).

Finally, if all regional groups do not follow the same policies and norms, and move in different ways, tension between them may become inevitable. If, for example, tightening of immigration control in one region, (e.g., western Europe) becomes more stringent, migration flows are likely to be diverted to the group or groups (e.g., North American region), which offer the easiest access., creating inter-regional tensions.

An absolute reliance on regional cooperation to manage global migration assumes that a perfect matching of push and pull factors driving migration can be achieved and a stable migration equilibrium maintained within each major reginal grouping. This however is hardly a realistic assumption, given that migration today is clearly a global process. (see also the discussion above concerning intra-regional movements). Movements of people do not stop at the frontiers of their respective regions. Nor is it possible to contain the pressure of emigration within the limits of a given region.

Indeed, it is difficult to imagine how the pressure for emigration can be absorbed within the confines of each specific region. The configuration and dynamics of modern migration defy such a tidy geographical arrangement.

Let us assume, by stretching our imagination, that through cooperative efforts the countries in the Americas achieve success in working out a stable equilibrium between emigration pressures and immigrant intakes within the American region itself and that countries in Eastern and Western Europe do the same within the European region.

By stretching our imagination further let us also assume, however unrealistically, that the flows from North Africa, too, are accommodated within a Euro-Mediterranean regional framework. Questions will still be remaining such as: What about all the peripheral countries in sub-Saharan Africa? How to accommodate the mounting emigration pressure from South Asia? Will even a wide, non-contiguous regional framework embracing Australia, New Zealand and the Gulf States be able to cope with it? In short, will not the intra-regional migration asymmetry—between emigration pressure and opportunities for legal entry—try to defy, possibly with the aid of human traffickers, the regional boundaries, even if these are defined in a flexible manner?

The regional approach suffers from other shortfalls as well. Regional and sub-regional arrangements, like bilateral agreements, are ill-equipped to deal with the problem of third-party free riders—for instance, when a tax is levied on immigration to neutralise or reduce its negative externalities. On the other hand, if they become restrictive fortresses, they tend to discriminate against outsiders, and close off opportunities for cross-border bargaining over migration issues.

Another important shortcoming of the regional approach concerns the potential danger that different regions may apply rules for admission and protection of migrants. In such a situation migration flows are most likely to be diverted to the region which has the most liberal migration regime, or which has the least effective immigration control. Also, as for the countries which may not belong to any regional grouping or and may have least effective control, they could well turn into a vast dumping ground for all kinds of unwanted immigration, and thus become a source of international tension and instability.

For a regional system to work smoothly, policy coherence among member countries is no less essential than it is for a global regime. A few years ago, an event within the Nordic group of countries illustrated how its absence can cause internal tension and threaten solidarity even in a relatively small group of countries. In May 2002 Sweden accused Denmark of a "lack of solidarity" "after seeing a surge of asylum-seekers that it partly blamed on a tougher line on immigration taken by its neigbour" (*Financial Times*, 28 May 2002).

The discussion in this chapter has once more brought into focus the fact that international migration is a veritable global process and that its effective management calls for global action. This is also clearly reflected in the global scope of the two recent protocols dealing respectively with migrant struggling and human trafficking. What is true of these two essentially punitive and preventive measures on migration must also be so for the pro-active measures to ensure its effective management. The two sets of measures—punitive and pro-active—are complementary and must be designed to support each other. Policymakers should be alive to the fact that it is easier to rally support for punitive action against a widely recognised evil like human trafficking than to build support for positive and pro-active measures that are, by nature, multifaced and have many stakeholders and ramifications.

The need for a global framework, based on a set of common principles and norms, for cooperative and harmonised inter-state action, as discussed in this chapter, does not imply that regional initiatives are irrelevant or useless.

On the contrary, the latter could be valuable building blocs for developing a global framework for better management of migration, providing however that a common global frame of reference is used to harness the regional efforts, avoiding the risk of confusion or friction between parallel regional initiatives, [and shunning the problem of third-party free riders.]

Indeed, regional and sub-regional consultations are extremely useful as inputs to the process of developing global norms in cases where these are still lacking. Global efforts can also draw support and inspiration from existing *best practices* as recognised at the regional/sub-regional levels. This can be combined with an issue-specific or modular approach—reaching global agreement on specific issues (e.g., return and readmission, portability of social security benefits) without ignoring the inter-linkage of issues and comprehensiveness of the regime.

In 1994 Barry Eichengreen and Peter Kenen advocated a similar composite approach in managing trade and monetary issues and succinctly narrated the merits a global framework for concerted action and the drawbacks of an exclusively regional or functional approach: (Eichengreen, B. and Kenen, P. 1994).

> ...proximity...does not always create a community of interests, and the quest for deeper integration may lead to a second solution—namely, functional rather than regional groups. But functional groups like regional groups, tend to discriminate against outsiders and close off opportunities for cross-issue bargaining. This is a reason for shunning them, or at least ensuring the compatibility with a third solution, adapting and strengthening the global institutional framework and insisting that both regional and functional negotiations take place within that framework.[4]

As in the case of trade, if all the regional groups move in the same direction within a global framework, they could serve as building blocs for an agreement on global migration, and the efforts could be complementary to, and supportive of, each other, combining the advantages of both "bottom up" and "top down" approaches. For this to happen they must move in the same direction, interlocked by shared objectives and common principles. However, there is clearly a potential danger that they may move in different directions, in which case instead of being building blocks they would become stumbling blocs.

References

Eichengreen, B., and P. Kenen. 1994. Managing the world economy under the Bretton woods system: An overview. In *Managing the world economy*, ed. Peter Kenen, 54. Washington, DC: Institute for International Economics.

[4] 'Managing the World Economy under the Bretton Woods System: An Overview', 1994. Institute for International Economics, Washington. D.C.

EUROSTAT, European Commission. "Demographics of the European Union", Luxembourg 2002.

Financial Times, London, 28 May 2002.

Ghosh, B. 2003. *Elusive protection, uncertain lands: Migrants' access to human rights*. Geneva: IOM.

Goodwin-Gill, Guy S. 2000. Migration: International law and human rights. In *Managing migration: Time for a new international regime?* ed. Bimal Ghosh. Oxford: Oxford University Press.

UNFPA, Executive Summary. 1998. *Technical symposium on international migration and development*, 34. The Hague, June–July 1998.

3

Attempts at Reaching a Multilateral Agreement on Migration: A Synoptic History

Spurred by the increasing need to manage migration through inter-state cooperation, nations have long tried to have a global agreement on migration, but for the reasons discussed in the previous two chapters, the road has been bumpy, and progress slow. The complexity and sensitivity of the issue of human mobility also explains, at least in part, why nations have found it more useful and convenient to have agreed rules on the cross-border movements of goods, services and capital than on human mobility. In 1992 Louis Sohn and Thomas Buergenthal wrote:

> The preoccupation of many governments with international trade in goods and service movements across national border has resulted in an elaborate set of international rules on that commercially important subject. Less attention has been paid to the development of rules governing the movement of human beings across national borders.[1]

[1] This applies mainly to openness for movement of people.

See also Ghosh B, "Introduction" *in Managing Migration: Time for a New International Regime*? Oxford University Press, 2000, pp. 1–5.

B. Ghosh, *The 2018 Global Migration Compact*,
https://doi.org/10.1007/978-3-030-82863-9_3

Even so, a long series of efforts were made to have a global agreement on cross-border movements of people. Already in 1927 the League of Nations attempted at the adoption of an international convention "to facilitate and regulate international exchange of labour". But soon the Great Depression gripped the world and there was no follow up.

In 1947 the International Chamber of Commerce urged the United Nations to convene a world conference to simplify border control and facilitate movement of persons and goods.[2] A committee of experts was accordingly set up by the UN Economic and Social Council. However, nothing specific and definitive seemed to have come out of it (ICC 1947).

In the wake of the World War II several international organisations (e.g. ILO, OEEC [now OECD], EEC [now EU]) called for free movement of workers to help economic reconstruction and development. War-devasted and labour-short Europe desperately needed additional workers to accelerate the speed of reconstruction and development. It made several bilateral arrangements for what was supposed to be temporary labour immigrants initially from nearby countries like Turkey but subsequently also from far-off developing countries.

But by early 1970, jump in oil prices and rising tides of unemployment led nations to abandon these calls and they were replaced by the slogan of a "New international division of labour" or taking work (to labour-rich countries) where the workers are. The new slogan was: 'trade in place of migration'. However, with the collapse of the 1961–67 Tokyo round of trade liberalization, especially as concerns trade concessions to developing countries, the new initiative failed to take off.

In 1980 the Willy Brandt (North-South) Commission lamented "…while countries of immigration have been able to migrant flows to suit their needs, countries of emigration have been buffeted by fluctuations in the demand for migrant labour and in remittances, and they have lost their skilled and semi-skilled manpower which they badly needed". It then called "for a concerted, and more just and equitable framework to regulate international migration on the basis of the interests of the

[2] Letter dated 3 January 1947 from ICC president Winthrop Aldrich, to UN Secretary-General Trygve Lie.

countries concerned" (North-South Commission 1980)[3] Sadly, once more, nothing much happened.

In 1993, a report issued by the Trilateral Commission, *Migration Challenges in the New Era,* saw a clear and compelling need for developing a comprehensive migration regime to provide a viable international framework within which to manage migration pressures effectively (Meissner et al. 1993). In the following year Fred Bergsten, director of the Washington-based Institute of International Economics, echoed the feeling by arguing that the world needs an international migration regime. In the same year James Purcell Jr. then director-general of the International Organization for Migration argued for a new migration order to better manage population movements (IHT 1993), while economists like Thomas Straubhaar and Klaus Zimmerman were urging nations to adopt a General Agreement on Migration Policy on grounds of greater efficiency in the world economy and the benefits they can derive from it. (Straubhaar 1994).

The year 1993 also saw a major institutional approach to the issue, with the Commission on Global Governance,[4] endorsing a detailed proposal (put forward by this author) for a new international regime to make migration safe, orderly and more predictable and manageable. This led to a project, dubbed NIROMP, (New International Regime for Orderly Movement of People), supported by the UN, and several West European governments, and was executed by the IOM, and directed by this author. It was the first comprehensive approach to cooperative management of global migration, with a clear configuration of its structure, based on commonality of objectives, harmonised normative principles and coordinated institutional arrangements.

In September 1997, the approach, hailing the principle of *regulated openness, and seeking a dynamic equilibrium between emigration pressure in origin countries and opportunities for legal entry in destination countries* was discussed at an intergovernmental meeting in Geneva, which generally endorsed the project's concept and objectives. It was then debated in a

[3] North-South-A Program for Survival, The MIT Press, Cambridge, Mass 02142,USA pp. 108–112.

[4] Co-chaired by Ingvar Carlsson, then Swedish prime minister and Shridath Ramphal, former secretary general of the Commonwealth Secretariat.

series of meetings in some major capital cities and university centres and was endorsed and supported by several international and regional meetings, both inter-governmental and non-governmental. In September1999 a second intergovernmental meeting was held in Geneva to help develop, as part of the project, a common framework for return and reintegration of migrants. In the following year it found a regional echo in a west African ministerial conference on migration and development.

Although it thus evoked a positive response from governmental and other sources, including from professionals, scholars, and academics, political constraints remained and stood in the way of the project making a major impact on *policy making*. And, with a change in the top management of IOM, there was no effective follow-up of the project activities.

However, the year 2001 saw an important step in the same direction, when, in line with the NIROMP approach, the Swiss government launched the Bern Initiative to facilitate interstate co-operation in planning and managing migration, based on common interests and concerns. Following the first conference in Bern (Bern 1, July 2003). it held four regional workshops in 2004 to benefit from regional inputs. A second international conference (Bern II) was held in the same year to take into account the regional inputs. However, by that time the original thrust of the initiative was considerably diluted, with a shift away from its original collective and regulatory approach. The consequence was the adoption of an "agenda" for pursuing well-meaning goals for migration management. Meanwhile, with political changes in the country and transfer of key officials concerned in the government, further action came to a halt.

Meanwhile, the increasing awareness of the need for a more concerted and coherent approach to migration management led several independent international commissions to take up the challenge. This included the Commission on Human Security, sponsored by the government of Japan, 2001–2003, and the World Commission on the Social Dimension of Globalisation, organized by the ILO in 2004. Among other things, they re-echoed the calls made by NIROMP and original Bern Initiative for the development of an international framework for better management of global migration. The ILO formally adopted a plan of action, one component of which concerned the development of a non-binding multilateral framework for a rights-based approach to labour migration.

In 2005 the EU Council, under the British presidency, put forward the idea of a "balanced, global and coherent approach". This was however limited, in effect, to countries sending their migrants to the EU countries, and the emphasis was on reducing irregular immigration through agreements with the countries of origin.

Then came, also in 2005, the Global Commission on International Migration, set up by Switzerland, Sweden and several like-minded countries and encouraged by Kofi Annan, then UN secretary general. But the commission shied away from the idea of a harmonised international framework on the ground that the governments were not ready for it. In 2006, at its first High-level Dialogue on Migration and Development, the United Nations took up, among other things, the Commission report. But no action was taken, except a decision on the establishment of a Global Forum on Migration and Development (GFMD), but outside the UN's organizational framework. The GFMD, although a useful platform for sharing information and exchanging ideas, has no formal mandate and its agenda for its two-yearly sessions is fixed by the rotating host government, in consultation with others. It was thus not specifically geared to developing a formal global agreement on migration management. The only other concrete thing that happened was the creation in the UN secretariat the post of a special representative on migration.

The narrative above highlights the fact that, despite efforts over decades and a plethora of consultations and eloquent pronouncements, the governments and inter-governmental organisations had been pretty elusive about the adoption of a formal global agreement on migration.

The momentum however was not totally lost as several academic, professional and civil society organisations across regions continued to pursue the issue. For instance, the sixth annual conference of Canada-based International Metropolitan Project made it keynote theme, which this author had the privilege to address. Given the interest aroused in the issue, it revisited the topic at its ninth annual conference in Amsterdam. The 21-point Action Programme of the Hague Process on Refugees and Migration included a commitment to gathering support for developing a concerted global approach to migration management. In the USA, Joel Trachtman, at Fletcher School of Law and Diplomacy, prepared the legal structure of a multilateral framework agreement to negotiate openness in labour migration (see annex). Ray Koslowski at the university of Albany executed, with the financial support of the MacArthur foundation, a project on global mobility regimes.

Finally, in 2018, a rare concurrence of events, including massive refugee and mixed migration flows, mainly from strife-torn MENA countries to western Europe and the Obama administration's pro-multilateral policies, led nations to meet at a summit in New York. It made a detailed declaration on making international migration safe and orderly and asked the United Nations to take up the matter and initiate further normative action. (discussed in Chap. 4 below).

Soon after this, in November 2019, following these waves of mixed migration and refugee flows to Europe, the G-20 leaders which had previously shunned the issue, got involved, and at its meeting in Antalya, Turkey, called upon governments to make collective efforts to improve capacity for managing migration and refuge flows and thus added its support to the New York Declaration. The G-20 message stressed the need for a coordinated and comprehensive response to the crisis and its consequences and to address the root causes of displacement (G-20 leaders' Communique 2015).

References

G-20 Leaders Communique Antalya Summit. 15–16 November 2015. http://europeansting.com/2015/11/16/g20live-g20-live

International Chamber of Commerce, Barriers to International Travel; *Report of its committee of experts for the simplification of formalities in international transport.* February 1947. Brochure no. 105.

Purcell, J.N. Jr. 1993. The world needs a policy for orderly migration. *International Herald Tribune*, 8 July 1993.

Meissner, D.M., et al. 1993. *International migration challenges in a new era.* New York: Trilateral Commission.

Straubhaar, T. 1994. Migration pressures. *International Migration* 31: 15–41.

4

The New York Declaration: As the Immediate Basis of the Compact

As mentioned in the previous chapter, a rare concurrence of events in 2015 paved the way, for the first time in history, to a comprehensive global agreement on migration. It was a year when the EU countries were swamped by huge and seemingly relentless waves of migration of more than one million people in a single year, with no signs of abating soon (Ghosh 2008). Aside from the magnitude of the flows, it was the rapid shifts in the routes, and modes of movements manoeuvred by the traffickers that made it difficult to manage the flows.

What added to Europe's predicament was the mixed composition of the flows—asylum-seekers, poverty-driven economic migrants and persons deserving humanitarian protection—all were bundled together, which made their screening and management both onerous and complex as well as time consuming. Also, unlike an orderly and planed process of family reunification, the arrival, not infrequently, of an entire family, with varying and urgent needs, including those of children, expectant mothers and elderly parents, made the management of the flows particularly complex and onerous.

Capping all these difficulties was the human agony in Europe and far beyond over the number of migrants' death in the Mediterranean on

B. Ghosh, *The 2018 Global Migration Compact*,
https://doi.org/10.1007/978-3-030-82863-9_4

their way to Europe. In 2015 the number of persons who died or disappeared in the Mediterranean rose to nearly 4600.

But if the situation in Europe was poignant and alarming, it also spurred inter-state solidarity. In the USA, the Obama administration's pro-multilateral policy was particularly sensitive to the urgency of a joint response to the situation in Europe, laying down the ways to deal with it and explore the ways of, if possible, avoiding its recrudescence in future. The prevailing cordial relation between Germany and the USA, too, played its part in initiating a joint international action at the highest possible political level, and using the United Nations System.

The heads of state and government accordingly met on 19 September 2016 for due deliberation, and the outcome was the "New York Declaration for Refugees and Migrants", expressing the political will of world leaders to protect the rights of migrants and refugees, save lives in peril related to mobility and share responsibility for better management of movements, especially large ones, on a global scale and laying the basis for the adoption of a global compact for safe, orderly and regular migration in 2018. It should be noted however that the declaration does not purport to establish any new obligations on UN member states (Aleinikoff, 2016).[1]

They also sought to develop guidelines on the treatment of migrants in vulnerable situations and achieve a more equitable sharing of the responsibility for managing migration and refugee flows.[2] More specifically, these objectives include:

- Protect the human rights of all refugees and migrants, regardless of status. This includes the rights of women and girls and promotion of their full, equal and meaningful participation in finding solutions and explore opportunities.
- Ensure that all refugee and migrant children are receiving education within a few months of their arrival in the host country.
- Prevent and respond to sexual and gender-based violence.
- Support those countries rescuing, receiving and hosting large numbers of refugees and migrants.

[1] Though it is not legally irrelevant (see Chapter 5, pg 49).

[2] The specific issue of refugee flows is not discussed in this book.

- Work towards ending the practice of detaining children for the purposes of determining their migration status.
- Strongly condemn xenophobia against refugees and migrants and support a global campaign to counter it.
- Strengthen the positive contributions made by migrants to economic and social development in their host countries.
- Improve the delivery of humanitarian and development assistance to those host countries most affected, including through innovative multilateral financial solutions, with the goal of closing all funding gaps.

4.1 Critical Appraisal of the Declaration

Positive Elements

The declaration is mostly, though not exclusively, a reiteration of the provisions in the already existing international laws and regulations on migration and refugees and is also by nature hortatory. Even so, it will be wrong to underrate its salience and relevance. The declaration provides a compilation of most of the principal legal provisions relevant to safe and orderly migration, including protection of migrants' rights and promotion of their welfare; this in itself is useful.

Additionally, by extending these provisions in new ways and directions and attuning them to more recent migratory issues and developments, including large and less predictable flows, it enhances its timeliness. The following are among the positive and specific elements in the declaration:

- It reiterates as a basic fact that migration today is a global process, calling for global solutions. Given that migration has become an integral part of globalisation, this should be pretty obvious. Yet this bears reiteration, given that there are countries which would still prefer to rely more on bilateral or even unilateral policies to deal with migration issues.
- It seeks to promote international cooperation on border control as an important element of state security, including for battling transnational organised crime, human trafficking and migrant smuggling,

terrorism and illicit trade, and acknowledges a shared responsibility to manage migration in a humane and sensitive manner It emphasises, in particular, the need for close cooperation among countries of origin, transit and destination.

- Though not new, this and other provisions recognising the rights and responsibilities of the states to manage and control their borders, consistent with international law, are useful as many governments are genuinely, though wrongly, fearful that international cooperation on migration is an infringement on state sovereignty or they use it as pretext for withholding their cooperation in managing migration. (see Chap. 2).
- It seeks to protect, in keeping with international law, human rights and fundamental freedoms of all migrants and refugees, regardless of their status. and reaffirms that they are entitled to due process in assessing their legal status, including in respect of entry and stay.
- It expresses its determination to deal with unsafe movements, especially irregular movements and to combat the exploitation, abuse and discrimination suffered by many migrants.
- It calls upon states that have not done so to consider ratifying or acceding to the 1990 UN Convention on the Protection of the Rights of All Migrant Workers and their Families and the relevant ILO Conventions. The special importance of the instrument stems from the fact that, for the first time, it clearly defines and specifically extends the basic human rights to all migrant workers and their families.
- Given that, under national laws, the primary concern is to protect and promote the rights and welfare of nationals, it is hardly surprising that, unless specifically protected under national law and practice, migrants as foreigners remain vulnerable relative to the nationals of a state. In a large number of countries, more than half of those included in a 1999 survey, constitutional and other domestic legal provisions against discrimination only apply to nationals. (ILO 1999)

However, although the call comes from the highest political level, it is uncertain what practical effect it is going to have on the situation, given some of the basic constrains involved and its history. It took more than 12 years since the adoption of the 1990 Convention to secure the minimum 20 ratifications required to make it operational. Some 31 years have elapsed since the adoption of the convention in 1990, but to date it has been ratified by no more than some 22 states.

It also suffers from several shortcomings. Aside from refugees and stateless persons, covered under separate instruments, it fails to cover, among others, migrant students and trainees, seafarers, and workers on offshore installations. There is also the general problem that even when such instruments are duly ratified and national laws are brought in line with the international standards, they are not in all cases effectively enforced (Ghosh 2008). There is a growing dichotomy between states' expression of concern for migrants' rights on the global forum and their willingness and ability to do something about it "back home". In this specific case, the state's inability to intervene applies particularly to millions of migrant workers engaged in the shadow or underground economy, which often remains outside the legal purview and control of labour ministries, and its inspection services (further discussed below).

- The declaration recognises the urgency of saving human lives in danger, but at the same time it emphasises the importance finding long-term and sustainable solutions as otherwise lives will continue to be threatened by the same cause. Although the declaration came closely on the heels of the cusp of the 2017 migration crisis, including the deaths of large numbers of migrants in transit, it is good that the declaration does not deal exclusively with the urgency of saving human lives, but takes a more balanced approach, combining the urgency of saving lives and exploring long-term and sustainable solutions.
- it re-emphasises the importance of fighting racism and xenophobia against migrants. Although this, too, is a call, which is by no means new, it assumes special importance as it comes from the highest political leaders and closely on the heels of some ugly racial incidents in several countries. But it does not speak of any new avenues of action or throw any new light on the issue.
- It pledges support to combat human trafficking and migrant trafficking and agrees to implement the United Nations Global Plan of Action to combat trafficking in persons, especially women and children. It also encourages states to accede, ratify and implement the United

Nations Convention against Transnational Organised Crime and the two related protocols.

- It needs to be noted however the these instruments are not free from criticism. Though they are essentially preventive and punitive in nature, they mandate states to protect and assist the victims, including for their physical, psychological and social recovery. Even so, NGOs have been somewhat critical of them on the grounds that they are biased towards anti-crime measures, and not sufficiently sensitive to the human rights of the victims. For instance, provision of assistance to victims have been left more to the discretion of authorities rather than a formal obligation. Concern has also been expressed that that the emphasis on anti-trafficking may undermine the position of those seeking refugee status, the latter being exposed to the potential risk of being given the status of victims of trafficking with fewer guarantees than those accorded to recognised refugees.
- It is particularly sensitive to the needs and vulnerabilities of child migrants, especially, unaccompanied children and those separated from their parents. It recognises that detention for child migrants, for purposes of verification of their migration status is seldom in the best interest of the child.
- This is also a timely reminder to stop the practice of detaining child migrants for unusually long periods of time and not necessarily in ideal conditions. In the USA, an official report revealed that a record number of 69, 550 migrant children were held in the detention centres in 2019, with as many as 60,000 for 40 days. The importance and poignance of the situation are enhanced by the fact, that the children were found to suffer 'inhuman and cruel experience in custody', as reported by Americans for Immigrant Justice. In the 2020 fiscal year migrant children spent an average of 102 days in federal government custody. More recently, given the surge of arrivals of child migrants in the first quarter of 2021, the Biden administration had opted for using the ill-famous emergency facility in Carrizo, triggering widespread concerns and criticisms.
- It ensures that all migrant children receive education within a few months of arrival and reaffirms that in dealing with child migration it

is the interest and rights of the child as enshrined in the international convention would serve as the pivotal factor and guiding principle.

- It also affirms that children should not be criminalised or subject to punitive measures because of their migration status or that of their parents, although it does not mention two specific problematic situations, as for example. in the USA children brought illegally by their parents into to the receiving country or children born in its territory but of illegal parents.
- As in the case of child migrants, it is sensitive to the vulnerability of women and girls and their specific needs and conditions. It seeks to prevent and respond to sexual and gender-based violence, avoid discrimination and brings into focus the importance of making full, equal and meaningful use of their participation in the development of local solutions and exploring opportunities.
- On average, women constitute nearly half (48%) of the total number of migrants. But their potential often remains un- or underutilised. Experience shows while under-utilisation of migrant' talents and skills or "de-skilling" is quite common, highly skilled women migrants are among the worst suffers.
- It recognises the importance of active participation of the private sector, and civil society, including migrant organisations in a multi-stakeholder alliance to support efforts to implement the declaration, including the commitments made in it.

4.2 Shortfalls and Deficiencies

The declaration is primarily designed to be comprehensive in response to the exigencies of "large" flows as Europe faced in 2015–6. But it fails to come up with a precise definition of the concept. It recognises that the term may be understood to reflect a number of considerations, including the number of people arriving, the economic social and geographical context, the capacity of a receiving state to respond to that is sudden or prolonged. And, it adds, almost as an afterthought, that large movements may involve mixed flows of people. It also seeks to make a distinction between "normal" and "large" flows.

But it fails to give a precise definition it applies in making the declaration and leaves the matter hanging. If the declaration (and the Compact) and the commitments in it are to be a guide for dealing with future large flows, it is almost essential to provide a definition of the term. As mentioned above, it was the unprecedentedly massive flows to EU countries in 2015/16 that provided the context of the declaration. Elsewhere, I have tried to discern the distinctive features of the 2015/2016 inflows to Europe. Briefly these are: the magnitude of the flows and the relative unpreparedness of destination countries and their limited absorptive capacity; the number of deaths of migrants in transit; rapid shifts in the routes and movement manoeuvred by the traffickers; mixed migration and family composition of the flows.

The declaration would have gained in its operational value had it specified, on the basis of some of these elements—including those already mentioned in the declaration—a set of criteria to take into account when determining what constitutes "large flows", in each case leaving it to the United Nations or IOM to announce, following due process, a flow as a "large" one.

A most important positive feature of the declaration is that it adheres to a balanced approach in addressing the root causes of current migration malaise. Just as it deals with the issue of treatment of immigrants in destination/transit countries, it also addresses the root causes of forced, irregular and disruptive emigration in origin countries. As already emphasised in Chap. 1, a well-managed migration system needs to address the problems and issues at both ends of the flow, which are also largely intertwined. If the pressure for disorderly, disruptive and forced migration in the origin countries are not effectively addressed, the destination countries, fearful of the situation and bereft of confidence in the system, are most likely to be both unwilling and unable to protect the rights of migrants on their territory or promote their welfare.

The declaration does well in making repeated references to the need for addressing the root causes of forced and disruptive emigration in the countries of origin. For instance, it announces 'we will address movements caused by instability, marginalization, and exclusion, and the lack of development and economic opportunities, with particular reference to the most vulnerable populations. we will work with countries of origin to strengthen their capacities'. (para. 2). 'It [2030 Agenda for Sustainable Development] will address many of the root causes of forced displacement, helping to create more favourable conditions'. 'We are determined to realize the full potential of that Agenda for refugees and migrants' (para 17). 'We favour an approach to addressing the drivers and root causes of large movements ....which would, *inter alia*, reduce vulnerability, combat poverty, improve self-reliance and resilience, and ensure a strengthened humanitarian-development nexus....' (para 37). 'We will analyse and respond to factors, including in countries of origin, which lead to, or contribute to large movements—Migration should be a choice, not a necessity' (para 43).

These are eloquent and lofty declarations, and though ambitious, they are timely and highly relevant. But they also imply tall orders. What is missing is a price tag to be attached to them and it is disappointing that, aside from a general reference to the implementation of the 2030 Sustainable Development Programme, there is no precise indication of the amount involved or where the essential wherewithal will come from. There are some indications of the sources of financing to meet the host country needs (para.38) but none for the origin countries. Given its importance, and to avoid repetition, the issue is further discussed in the next chapter, including the creation of a start-up fund to jump start a specific project.

References

Aleinikoff, T.A. 2016. The UN refugee summit: What can be achieved? ag.

Ghosh, B. 2008. *Human rights and migration: The missing link.* Utrecht: University of Utrecht.

ILO. International Labour Conference *Migrant Workers* Geneva, 1999.

5

The 2018 Global Compact on Migration

The compact, which is basically a reaffirmation of the New York Declaration and builds upon it, has 23 main objectives as follows (See box below):

Objectives for Safe, Orderly and Regular Migration

1. Collect and utilise accurate and disaggregated data as a basis for evidence-based policies.
2. Minimise the adverse drivers and structural factors that compel people to leave their country of origin.
3. Provide accurate and timely information at all stages of migration.
4. Ensure that all migrants have proof of legal identity and adequate documentation.
5. Enhance availability and flexibility of pathways for regular migration.
6. Facilitate fair and ethical recruitment and safeguard conditions that ensure decent work.
7. Address and reduce vulnerabilities in migration.
8. Save lives and establish coordinated international efforts on missing migrants.
9. Strengthen the transnational response to smuggling of migrants.
10. Prevent, combat, and eradicate trafficking of persons in the context of international migration.

(*continued*)

B. Ghosh, *The 2018 Global Migration Compact*,
https://doi.org/10.1007/978-3-030-82863-9_5

(continued)

11. Manage borders in an integrated, secure, and coordinated manner.
12. Strengthen certainty and predictability in migration procedures for appropriate screening, assessment, and referral.
13. Use migration detention only as a measure of last resort and work towards alternatives.
14. Enhance consular protection, assistance, and cooperation throughout the migration cycle.
15. Provide access to basic services for migrants.
16. Empower migrants and societies to realise full inclusion and social cohesion.
17. Eliminate all forms of discrimination and promote evidence-based public discourse to shape perceptions of migration.
18. Invest in skills development and facilitate mutual recognition of skills.
19. Create conditions for migrants and diasporas to fully contribute to sustainable development in all countries.
20. Promote faster, cheaper, and safer transfer of remittances and foster financial inclusion of migrants.
21. Cooperate in facilitating safe and dignified return and readmission as well as sustainable reintegration.
22. Establish mechanisms for the portability of social security entitlements and earned benefits.
23. Strengthen international cooperation and global partnerships for safe, orderly, and regular migration.

The compact was approved by 164 members. However, despite the importance of the subject, the timeliness of the endeavour, and the non-binding nature of the agreement, the Compact seems to have failed to evoke an enthusiastic reaction or universal support.

Some 33 countries failed to adhere to the agreement. This included one-third of EU member states, although the EU Parliament was in favour of the agreement and had issued a declaration to that effect. The EU found itself divided at home, divided abroad. The countries that refrained from approving include: Australia, Bulgaria, the Czech Republic, Croatia, Estonia, Hungary, Israel, Italy, Poland, Slovakia, Slovenia, Switzerland and the USA. Twelve countries abstained.

The nature of the reservations or the tone of criticisms varied, depending on the country-specific situations and ideological bias of the ruling government, political parties and other groups concerned.

Some were fearful that family reunification for migrants at all skill levels will dampen meritocratic immigration systems currently in practice in several countries. The US state department was scornful of the provisions to police speech that could be interpreted as xenophobic on the ground that this could lead to the infringement of free speech by repressive regimes that seek to suppress free speech. It also expressed reservations about the compact as it was perceived to constitute an infringement on state sovereignty. Austria felt that its "three-components policy—keeping power to decide migration policy at country level, more order and control, and cooperation with countries of origin—is more effective that the 'one size fits all" approach underlying the new Compact. In Belgium, the coalition government collapsed over the issue of signing the agreement. In Slovakia, it led to the resignation of its foreign minister. In Belgium, the coalition government collapsed over the issue of signing the Compact.

Some thought that the Compact has sharpened the dispute over immigration, has stiffened the opposition of right-wing, conservative governments and groups and has done more harm than good for the pro-immigration policies and activists.

On the other hand, many others felt that the agreement fell short of expectations over making migration safe, orderly and regular. The tone and language were too soft to match the ambitious objectives of the project, according to these critics. "It started with a sharp bang, but ended with a whimper," some of them thought.

Several of these negative reactions are clearly based on a misconceived understanding of the characteristics of the compact. For instance, it does not constitute an infringement on state sovereignty. It is more a catalogue of *best practices* and non-binding. Also, by voluntarily adhering to it, states can enrich its sovereign capacity to deal with extra-territorial or planetary issues like the Covid crisis or environmental degradation. It needs to be noted however that although the compact is legally non-binding, critically speaking, it is not legally irrelevant in as much as the courts may be willing to consider it as an aid to interpreting immigration legislation, as the Crown Law office in New Zealand opined.

Likewise, it is wrong to suggest that the compact frames migration as a human right, as some critics have done. It urges governments to respect human rights of immigrants in their territories just as they would like to see their own emigrants abroad similarly treated. Indeed, many governments have already made commitments to respect basic human rights under international laws.

5.1 The Strength and Weakness of the Compact: Positive Elements

As with the New York declaration, the compact contains a number of positive elements related to safe and orderly migration, including:

(a) It lays emphasis on the beneficial effects of orderly migration (although it is less vocal to spell out the negative consequences of forced, disorderly, and irregular migration, as also mentioned below).
(b) Makes a clear recognition that international migration is a global process and needs a global approach to manage it.
(c) Lays emphasis on the need for a comprehensive approach to migration management and for the involvement of the whole government and the whole society, given the crosscutting issues involved. Migration management has long suffered because of a piecemeal approach, instead of a comprehensive one (further discussed in the next section below).
(d) Makes clear that the cooperative management of migration does not imply any infringement on national sovereignty and that the state has the prerogative to govern migration within its territory, in conformity with international law.
(e) Provides clarification that while saving human lives in danger is essential, so also is finding long-term and sustainable solutions as otherwise lives will continue to be threatened by the same cause.
(f) Denounces the shortfalls of the prevailing system of "responsibility by proximity" to manage overflows of migrants, although it is silent on any formal responsibility-sharing arrangement or structure by states beyond the neighbouring ones.

(g) Reiterates condemnation of racism and xenophobia.
(h) Makes migration management sensitive to the special needs of children and women and other vulnerable migrants.
(i) Seeks to lay emphasis on migrants' rights and welfare, including those related to family reunion, migrants' access to consular services of their countries, the portability of their social security benefits and safe and inexpensive ways of making remittances.

5.2 Confusing, Inadequate, or Missing Elements

While containing these positive elements, it also suffers from a number of ambiguities and shortfalls as summarised below:

1. The compact does the right thing by emphasising the importance of collecting data related to all aspects of migration as a basis for policy formulation. One of the nagging problems is the absence of uniformity in methods of data collection on migration and its definitions in different countries allowing easy comparability, which is critically important to support inter-state cooperation. It would have been useful to seek, with the help of the UN Statistical Commission, harmonisation of national methods of collecting migration data, without prejudice to states' sovereign rights to formulate their domestic migration policies,
2. Under the section "Our Vision and Guiding Principles," (para.8), the compact emphasises the positive contributions of (orderly and regular) migration, but, quite surprisingly, makes no mention of the negative consequences of forced, disorderly and irregular migration, which needs to be avoided.[1]

[1] In the section on *shared responsibilities* (paragraph 11) there is a passing reference to action needed for "reducing the incidence and negative impact of irregular migration" but this is only a passing reference and gives no indication as to how this is to be done.

In both rich and poor countries there are already millions of irregular migrants living in dark corners of the society. Marginalised, disgruntled and alienated, they could easily turn radical, embrace revengeful fundamentalism and become virulent agents of social violence and disruptions. It should not be forgotten that, aside from the existing stocks of irregular migrants, any large flows, with mixed composition are most likely to include irregular migrants.

Under the section "Our vision and Guiding Principles" the document aptly and eloquently refers to the enormous contributions that over the ages migration has made to human civilization. But it fails to mention the hardships, sacrifices and sufferings that too, not infrequently, had been associated with these movements. It would have been useful to add that the compact aims at reaping the potential positive contributions of future migration, while avoiding or mimising the perils and hardships of the past.

One wonders if at the very beginning of this section a powerful reference to the evils of forced and irregular migration, alongside the benefits of safe and regular migration, would not have strengthened the balanced approach that underlies the compact.

The lacuna makes the whole discourse less balanced and seemingly too partisan, which contributes to further polarization of the migration debate. The omission also makes the compact an easy prey to those critics who wrongly claim that it would open the floodgates of irregular migration and enable populist governments and others to use it as a pretext to shun the Compact altogether. Several other countries, including Austria and Bulgaria, thought the agreement blurs the lines between regular and irregular migration.

As part of remedial action against irregular migration it would have been useful to refer to the role that the rapidly expanding informal sector of the economy or black economy plays in feeding it.

In several rich countries sunset or declining industries and marginal firms are trying to survive by hiring cheap, docile and irregular immigrant, while avoiding payment of taxes. The demand increases during periods of economic decline. In the EU it accounted for only 5% of the GDP in 1970, it rose to 16% by late 1990s. At that time between 10 and 20 million workers, mostly, though not exclusively, irregular migrants were engaged in this sector, and their numbers seem to have been rising since then. (European Commission 1998, Ghosh 1998 *Financial Times* 8 April, 1989 *International Herald Tribune* 10 June 1998). What is particularly disturbing is that even some of the respectable companies, including fashion houses in the organised sector, are now taking advantage of the situation through sub-contracting arrangements with firms operating in the black economy. (Contini 1982; Weiss 1987).

As discussed, "large" is an imprecise and term, and, as it recognizes, it is relative to the nature of the flow and the country-specific situations at both ends. A "large movement" would not include "normal and regular flows from one country to another". However, the Declaration and the compact cover both and the distinction becomes blurred at times.

The compact's main, almost exclusive, concern relates to the urgency created by large flows of migration. Although it makes reference to natural disasters, climate change and environmental degradation, it ignores other kinds of migration-related urgencies, such as exigencies created by COVID 19. The pandemic has created a genuine need for imposing certain travel restrictions, but there is a serious potential risk that autocratic governments will take advantage of the situation and maintain for long the unduly restrictive policies and measures, even after the pandemic dies down. To avoid abuse or confusion it would have been useful to lay down the conditions, including the duration of a justifiable temporary suspension of the relevant provisions of the compact, in the event of a genuine emergency.

Given that the compact's whole-of-society approach, one wonders if the compact would not have gained if it would have also made a reference to the relationship between trade and emigration pressure in poor, origin countries. The slogan in mid-1970s of "trade in lieu of migration" may have lost some of its lustre in view of the collapse of the Tokyo Round of trade of liberalisation and subsequent tensions in world trade, but its essence remains valid. If rich countries place undue restrictions (physical barriers or heavy import duty) on poor countries' labour-intensive goods in which they may have a comparative advantage, this will add to the pressure for emigration through regular or irregular channel, and defeat objective 2 of the compact itself.

Although the compact emphasises the importance of a comprehensive approach, it fails to follow it through, and makes no specific reference to the close inter-linkage between different types of the flow. As experience shows, when one channel of movement does not work properly, it also adversely affects the functioning of other channel or channels as the flows are diverted to the latter, burdening and clogging their smooth operation. In the past the UNHCR has complained that the restrictions on labour immigration, despite unmet labour demand in destination countries, were driving potential labour migrants to try the asylum-seeking channel and thus clogging it. Or they seek entry through irregular channels.

The situation involves "category jumping" by prospective migrants and asylum seekers and creates the problem of "mixed migration" which, in turn, makes it difficult to screen and manage the flows.

To illustrate, in Western Europe, a ban on labour immigration in 1973–74 accelerated family reunification—as reflected, in particular, in the increased outflows from Turkey to Germany post 1973—and it also increased irregular migration. When governments tightened restrictions on irregular migration, it coincided with a sharp rise in asylum-seeking from an annual average of 16,000 to in the first half of the 1970s to 200,000 in 1986–87 and around 700,000 in 1991. As policies were focussed on limiting asylum-seeking, alongside a small decline in asylum-seeking, irregular migration, including human trafficking, started rising again. These coincidences of events, even if they do not prove direct causal relationships, underscore the inadequacies of a fragmentary approach, and the need for a comprehensive and coherent one for sound migration management.

Much of the recent large movements are from strife-torn MENA countries. The Compact makes a pious exhortation in urging nations to put an end to armed conflicts. This is fine, but those directly concerned with migration, including the ministries concerned, cannot do much about it, though they can lend support to heads of government. A modest but practical proposal would have been to make it an obligation for the states to carry out, as part of the planning of any kind of lawful military intervention, a projected assessment of the migration implications of the up-coming intervention and make anticipatory arrangements to deal with it.

The Compact is a legally non-binding agreement or a soft international instrument. As I have argued elsewhere, this is unavoidable. The question of state sovereignty apart, given the wide range of issues involved, the distinctive characteristics of each major type of flow and their respective situations, the agreement does not lend itself to be treated as a hard instrument.

However, the Compact could have gained in efficacy and impact had it laid more emphasis on two elements. First, the implementation and the efficacy of a soft instrument depends critically on the ethical value people attach to it. (The Universal Declaration on Human Rights is a case in point). Civil society holds the potential of playing a crucial role in mobilizing such societal support and strengthening people's attachment to it. The compact aptly makes a general reference to the role of the private sector and the civil society for its implementation.

However, it falls short of spelling out some specific ways, including provision of facilities and inducements, of enabling and encouraging civil society (migrants associations, human rights organisations and the like) to play its role in strengthening and mobilising popular support to the ethical base of the state-led agreement. Likewise, it would have been useful to give some leads on how the private sector can play its part in job creation, including through techno-economic research to identify viable new economic activities.

Second, as a follow-up, the compact aptly mentions the importance of its application and review at national, sub-regional and regional levels, cementing its spatial or vertical integration. But it ignores the fact that the compact also opens a window of opportunity for additional, complementary normative action, including adoption of both hard and soft instruments, depending on the nature of the issues involved.

Each of such instruments should be fully attuned to the broad objectives and principles of the overall compact. The arrangement will thus take the form of a mosaic of autonomous but interrelated instruments geared to the common objectives and principles of the Compact.

Such complementary instruments include bilateral and plurilateral agreements on return and readmission of migrants and agreements on exchange of skills under labour migration based on reciprocity. On the latter, Joel Trachtman at the Fletcher School of Law and Diplomacy has drawn up the structure of a multilateral framework for labour migration, under which states could freely negotiate commitments in exchanging skills, based on reciprocity of interests and unlock mutual and global welfare gains. (see Annex II) This fits well into the overall framework of the compact. The interlocking of the two approaches within the common framework should constitute a critical nexus needed to ensure coherence and effectiveness of migration management.

The Compact rightly underlines the importance of the protection of migrants' rights and promotion of their welfare. For both temporary and especially for long-term/settlement migrants, these are critically important. But these should not be perceived in conflictual terms or as a one-way issue. For long-term/settlement migrants, these are essential elements of meaningful integration in which both migrants' rights and their obligations are intertwined. The compact hardly speaks of migrant integration as a two-way process involving the host society and the migrants.

It focuses on large flows and refers to return and readmission, but it hardly makes any distinction between different types of migration in terms of duration of stay, for instance—between settlement migration and temporary migration, including circular and border migration. While the basic human and migrants' rights and obligations are of importance to all of them, their specific needs, conditions and obligations vary in many ways.

For settlement migration it is important to lay down certain principles and arrangements that enable them to participate in, and contribute to the host society, its economy and its culture thus enhancing the all-around benefits of migration, as the compact aims at (Ghosh 2005a, b, c).

The host society, for its part, is entitled to expect that the migrants would have an understanding of, and respect for, the laws and traditions of the host society. This implies a two-way process of attitudinal and cultural adjustment between nationals and migrants. A real challenge here concerns migrants' equal partnership in the larger host society and the possibility of their continuing links with their communities of origin.

Given the increasing importance of temporary migration and a growing trend of advocacy in its favour, it would have been timely if the compact would have given some consideration to it.

References

Contini, B. 1982. The second economy. In *The underground economy in the United States and abroad*, ed. V. Tanzi.

European Commission. 1998.

Ghosh, B. 1998. Tame Europe's black economy in international Herald Tribune, 10 June 1998.

———. 2005a. Economic effects of international migration: A synoptic overview. In *World migration report, 2005, costs and benefits of international migration*. IOM.

———. 2005b. The challenge of integration: A global perspective. In *Managing integration*, ed. Rita Sussmuth and Werner Weidenfeld.

———. 2005c. Managing migration: Interstate cooperation at the global level: Is the emergence of a new paradigm of partnership around the corner?

Weiss, L. 1987. Explaining the underground economy: State and social structure. *British Journal of Sociology* 38.

6

What Makes the Compact Incomplete and Lopsided

Aside from these deficiencies, what makes the compact seriously incomplete concerns the inadequate follow-up and weak commitment related to the compact's own objective no.2 which deals with the pressure of irregular and disruptive emigration in origin countries.

It thus fails to fully answer such fundamental questions as: Why are existing migration flows so often forced, unsafe and irregular and take place not as a matter of free choice? Why do destination countries fail to protect the rights of migrants and safeguard their welfare already enshrined in existing national laws and international instruments? Little is said about these root causes in countries of origin.

6.1 Effective Management of Migration Needs Action at Both Ends of the Flow

The discussions in previous chapters have recurrently revealed that effective management of migration needs action at both ends of the flow (without ignoring the paths of the movement and the transit countries). As regards the destination countries, the compact aptly deals with the

B. Ghosh, *The 2018 Global Migration Compact*,
https://doi.org/10.1007/978-3-030-82863-9_6

question of openness of entry just as it is eloquent and extensive in seeking to protect the rights and welfare of the migrants. But it ignores the specific measures that needs to be taken concurrently to tame the pressure of forced and disorderly migration in the origin/source countries: a task clearly embedded in objective 2 of the compact.

Such action will be helpful to promote development, social peace and welfare in the origin countries themselves, but it would also encourage and help the destination countries to play their role in protecting the rights of migrants and safeguarding their welfare. They will have more confidence in the system. They will have the feeling that the system is working, and the flows are becoming manageable. In turn, they will feel encouraged and be in a better position to safeguard the rights and welfare of the migrants on their soil.

The absence of a robust confidence among the destination countries in the present migration management system explains at least in part their relative indifference to existing (and in many cases already accepted and ratified) laws concerning the protection of rights and welfare of migrants.

Under objective no.2 of the compact, the states are committed "to minimize the drivers and structural factors that compel people to leave their country." Elsewhere, it wants migration to be a matter of "choice, not a necessity." But, aside from reiterating some generalities, such as sustainable development, increased investment, peace-making and preparedness, there is no specific action plan, no specific structure and, unlike, for example, the EU/Africa partnership agreement, no allocation of adequate funds to address the root causes of irregular and disorderly migration in origin countries, except a very modest multi-partner trust fund (discussed below).

It is useful to recall, that as a follow-up to its Valletta Action Plan (2015), the EU envisaged an increase in the resources of its Africa Trust Fund by EUR 500 million, which it had already set up for this purpose with an initial capital of EUR 1.9 billion. Additionally, the EU dangled a pot of EUR 3.4 billion in guarantees for private investment, backed by a further EUR 3.4 billion from member states for countries willing to sign agreements with the EU on migration. It also envisaged the possibility of raising a total of EUR 88 billion through leveraging.

Several of these projections seemed too optimistic and have remained yet to be fully realised. Even so, they are indicative of the resources needed to make an impact on stemming the root causes of disruptive and irregular migration.

In the USA, too, recent administrations have sought to stem large, disruptive migratory flows, including waves of child migrants, by using aid resources to attack their root causes in three Central American Countries (dubbed "Northern Triangle"). In January 2015 president Obama had proposed US$ 1-billion aid programme for improving the economic and security situation in these countries. Although initially only $ 300 million was made available mainly for security, US Congress subsequently approved an additional $ 750 million for the whole programme.

Recently, President Biden, (who as vice president in the Obama administration piloted much of the negotiations with the Central American leaders) has called for his country to provide $ 4 billion to the origin countries in Central America for addressing the root causes of massive and disorderly emigration flows.

Although programmes of this kind hold significant promise, the two recent programmes—for Africa and Central America—show only mixed results (see Coggio 2021 and Ghosh 2008, respectively). Given the complexity of these programmes which are multi-faceted, involve multiple actors and by nature take time for fruition, this is not surprising.

The success of any such programme depends largely on two basic conditions: (i.) a clear definition of its scope and objectives; and (ii) genuine conviction, mutual trust and commitment of both parties to its effective implementation.

As regards the programme objectives, these should not be widely dispersed to cover the whole area of development but consistent with any such general development programmes, including the one of sustainable development (UNSDG), it must specifically aim to address the "adverse drivers and structural factors" that generate pressure for disorderly and irregular migration in origin countries. This should include development of any depressed or backward areas generating forced migration.

As for the commitment to the programme, origin countries must feel that they themselves *own* the programme and conceive it as a home-spun one and not imposed upon them by outsiders. The destination countries, for their part, must do all possible to avoid creating the feeling that it is an imposed programme.

Also, as part of their genuine confidence and commitment, origin countries must be convinced of the intrinsic merits of the programme and not simply attracted by the lure of the external aid money. Destination countries, for their part, must not seek to use it as a Trojan Horse to stem or stop emigration by promoting stay-at-home economic practices in origin countries.

In this context it is useful to recall the effects of development on migration. Contrary to the "hump theory" on the development-migration nexus, (*first more migration, and then falling and stable migration),* development does not shape only the levels of migration, but also, and more importantly, the composition of the flows.

A broad based and employment-oriented development programme would normally encourage and enable the movement of those potential migrants who seek better opportunities abroad and are guided by a more rational assessment of costs and benefits of the move. These opportunity-seeking migrants (discussed in Chapter 1, p. 3) are also less likely to take unsafe and irregular channels.

Development of this kind should also have a salutary, but subsidiary effect on reducing the number of forced or survival migrants. This latter effect will be enhanced when development is specifically targeted at the 'adverse drivers and other structural factors' that cause unsafe, disruptive and irregular migration.

True, the Compact does envisage the establishment of a start-up fund, dubbed multi-partner trust fund, to help make migration safe, orderly and regular. However, with the target of US $ 25 million for the first year of its operation, its resources portend to be far too modest and with its aim of facilitating the exchange on best practices and evidence-based migration policies, its ambit of action on the ground remains far too limited to make an impact on adverse drivers and structural factors that cause forced and disorderly migration.

Box 6.1 Multi-partner Start-Up Fund

Overview

There are an estimated 258 million international migrants, close to 3.4% of the world's population. 48% of them are women. The majority of migrants move between countries in a safe, orderly and regular manner, and migration itself is overwhelmingly positive for migrants and communities of origin, transit and destination. Yet migration when unregulated presents challenges for all communities, often leaving migrants vulnerable to abuse and exploitation. All this makes migration governance one of the most urgent and profound tests of international cooperation in our time.

The Start-Up Fund for Safe, Orderly and Regular Migration (or Migration MPTF) was called for by the *Global Compact on Migration*, adopted by the General Assembly in December 2018. It is a UN financing mechanism primarily to assist Member States in their national implementation of the Global Compact. UN entities at the country-level will work with national partners on identifying migration needs through joint analysis and on designing joint programmes to provide a collective response to those needs. The Migration MPTF supports the 23 objectives of the Global Compact and adheres to its 360-degree approach. The Migration MPTF will also provide funding to regional and global initiatives in support of the GCM implementation.

Strategic approach

The Migration MPTF is the only funding mechanism fully dedicated to supporting collective action on migration and ensuring that the mutual trust, determination and solidarity amongst States and with other stakeholders can be fostered to ensure safe, orderly and regular migration. Heeding the call of the Global Compact to be implemented at local, national, regional and global levels, the Migration MPTF is designed to support initiatives at all levels.

- **Guiding principles.** All its activities incorporate the 10 key guiding principles established by the Global Compact: (i) people-centred, (ii) international cooperation, (iii) national sovereignty, (iv) rule of law and due process, (v) sustainable development, (vi) human rights, (vii) gender-responsive, (viii) child-sensitive, (ix) whole-of-government approach, and (x) whole-of-society approach.
- **Funding.** Every country-specific request to the Migration MPTF is based on the relevant Member State's needs in implementing the Global Compact, with the prerequisite of their full endorsement of the support to be provided by the United Nations system and other stakeholders, as agreed upon during the consultation and design phase.

(*continued*)

Box 6.1 (continued)

- **Joint programming.** Each request for funding requires UN joint programming calling on the capacities and expertise of at least two UN entities, as well as partnership with local authorities and other non-UN stakeholders, including migrants and migrant organizations, where appropriate, in the design and implementation of programmes/projects.

The Migration MPTF is rooted in the 2030 Agenda for Sustainable Development and builds upon its recognition that migration is a multidimensional reality of major relevance to the sustainable development of countries of origin, transit and destination. The Fund will help realize the intrinsic link between the Global Compact on Migration and the achievement of all SDGs, in particular but not exclusively with respect to target 10.7 which calls on States to "facilitate orderly, safe and responsible migration and mobility of people, including through implementation of planned and well managed migration policy".

References

Coggio, T. 2021. "Europe's Tackling of Root Causes of African Migration had a Mixed Record". Source: Migration Information Source, MPI, Washington DC. 6 May 2021.

Ghosh, B. 2008. *Human rights and migration: The missing link*. Utrecht: University of Utrecht.

Conclusions: A Breathtaking Achievement or an Opportunity Lost or Both?

On the one hand, the compact is a significant breakthrough, as for the first time ever in migration history nations have agreed on a *comprehensive* arrangement to better manage global migration. The roadblock is lifted, and the ice is now broken, opening the possibility of taking further action at the global level to meet the remaining needs now and in future.

On the other hand, it is unfortunate that full advantage was not taken of an opportunity created by a rare concurrence of events to make the compact complete and more balanced, by giving more focussed attention, including making financial commitment, to addressing the root causes of the present migration malaise at the origin country end. The agreement is certainly not fake, it is real and promising, but incomplete and needs to be made more balanced, taking advantage of the International Migration Review, to be held every four years and charged with the responsibility of "building upon accomplishments and identifying opportunities for further action."

B. Ghosh, *The 2018 Global Migration Compact*,
https://doi.org/10.1007/978-3-030-82863-9

The long-term goal of making migration a matter of choice and not of compulsion should continue to be pursued and the push and pull factors driving global migration brought into a dynamic harmony. The journey has begun, and it is already more than half-way through; it is awaiting to be completed.

Annexes

Annex 1

Is migration management a dirty word?

Attempts to make international migration more orderly are not new. They go at least as far back as 1927 when the League of Nations sought to adopt a convention to facilitate and regulate international exchange of labour. But, as recently as the late 1980s, "managing migration" was perceived almost as a dirty word.

My initial writings introducing the concept of management of migration, in the wake of the fall of the Berlin wall in 1989 and in the early 1990s, had come under attack from two extremes. Libertarians, including liberal economists, disliked "management" as they believed in the free flow of people, with individuals to sell their skills or labour in the world market. The enthusiasts on state sovereignty and other 'restrictionists' were equally anxious to dump the word "management" because of their unflinching faith in unilateral control. "Management" was too soft a word to convey this sense.

I remember my experience during a ministerial level conference held in Dakar on migration in 2000. As the scientific coordinator of the ministerial conference, I may have used the term "management" and that

B. Ghosh, *The 2018 Global Migration Compact*,
https://doi.org/10.1007/978-3-030-82863-9

terribly upset the leader of a major European country. Why use "management" and not "control"; it dilutes the sense of control we would like to have on migration, he argued.

I tried to explain the concept of "management" by saying that the term indeed has a wider connotation, and added that "It is used in this context to signify a process by which two or more conflicting forces are brought into a dynamic harmony. What we are witnessing today in this arena, I i is a conflict between two powerful forces: rising emigration pressure on the one hand and dwindling opportunities for legal entry, especially for low skilled workers. Effective management of migration seeks to bring this mismatch into a dynamic equilibrium or harmony."

Why do this? I also explained that "unlike unilateral control, the concept of management is also related to a set of precise objectives: making movement of people more orderly and predictable as well as productive and humane based on a commonality and a reciprocity of interests of all the actors involved—sending and receiving and transit countries and the migrants themselves."

I do not know if I really convinced him but at least he did not make any further fuss at the conference as he had threatened to do.

Regulated Openness

A guiding principle and a critical element in migration management as I have defined is regulated openness. This term too could create some uneasiness for some people. I remember when I used this term in a 1997 NIROMP meeting, a representative of a migrant sending developing country expressed his concern saying "under the project we will certainly have plenty of regulation to restrict but very little openness". A typical rejoinder from a receiving country was "we are sure to have a lot of openness but very little regulation to restrain outflows". Both these fears are of course unfounded.

Regulated openness should not be conceived as a one-sided affair or one-way traffic. Full and effective enforcement of the principle calls for action at both ends of the flow. For instance, openness does not relate to, or involve the receiving countries alone. The possibility to leave one's own country can also be negated by a sending country, as the communist or command economy countries—and for certain type of migrants, a few developing countries—had done or tried to do in the past. Similarly, destination countries will be hard put to ensure and maintain openness in inflows unless sending countries play their part in regulating or restraining disorderly or irregular outflows.

Migration Management and Migration Governance

Migration governance is an overused, catch all phrase, conveniently used to mean many things for many different purposes. Loosely used and shorn of specificity, the term remains amorphous and elusive in articulating what it really stands for. It is therefore safe and innocuous. And this precisely may be the reason why the term has become quite popular, including in the migration literature.

The Commission on Global Governance, in the work of which I participated, was perhaps the first international body to delve deeply into the concept of governance. It defined governance as a broad, dynamic and complex process of interactive decision making that evolves to changing circumstances, but **it must take an integrated approach to human survival and prosperity**. In other words, it is a process, but it does not exist or operate in a vacuum. It is closely related to a product or specific goal or objective, even if the latter may change over time or vary according to the subject area.

Annex 2

Appendix 2: Illustrative Draft General Agreement on Labor Migration www.https://research.upjohn.org/hp-press

This illustrative draft agreement is provided merely to indicate the types of provisions that might be negotiated by states if they were to determine to enter into a multilateral "General Agreement on Labor Migration." Its provisions should be understood more as a checklist of issues to consider than as a recommendation as to how issues should be resolved. Furthermore, there are many additional issues that states will wish to consider as they approach such an agreement. Finally, this illustrative draft agreement does not contain provisions creating or specifying the design of an organization in which to house the agreement.

1. Preamble

   1.1. Recognizing the growing importance of migration for the growth and development of the world economy;
   1.2. Wishing to establish a multilateral framework of principles and rules for migration with a view to the expansion of migration under conditions of transparency and progressive liberalization and as a means of promoting the economic growth of all home states and destination states and the development of developing countries;
   1.3. Desiring the early achievement of progressively higher levels of liberalization of migration through successive rounds of multilateral negotiations aimed at promoting the interests of all participants on a mutually advantageous basis and at securing an overall balance of rights and obligations, while giving due respect to national policy objectives;
   1.4. Recognizing the right of Members to regulate, and to introduce new regulations, on the health standards applicable to immigrants, the security standards applicable to immigrants, and the qualifications of professions and skilled work within their territories;
   1.5. Desiring to facilitate the reduction of poverty and the development of developing countries;
   1.6. Taking particular account of the serious difficulty of the least-developed countries in view of their special economic situation and their development, trade and financial needs;

Hereby agree as follows:

Part I: Scope and Definitions

2. Scope. This Agreement applies to measures by member states affecting labor migration, including without limitation immigration.
3. Definitions

   3.1. For the purposes of this Agreement, labor migration is defined as the physical departure of a citizen of one Member from that Member, the travel of such citizen to a destination Member, and the admission and residence of such citizen in the destination Member, for the purpose of seeking or taking up any type of labor.
   3.2. For the purposes of this Agreement:

      3.2.1. "measures by Members" means measures taken by:

         3.2.1.1. central, regional or local governments and authorities; and
         3.2.1.2. nongovernmental bodies in the exercise of powers delegated by central, regional or local governments or authorities;

      3.2.2. In fulfilling its obligations and commitments under the Agreement, each Member shall take such reasonable measures as may be available to it to ensure their observance by regional and local governments and authorities and nongovernmental bodies within its territory.

Part II: 7 General Obligations and Disciplines

4. Transparency

   4.1. Each Member shall publish promptly and, except in emergency situations, at the latest by the time of their entry into force, all relevant measures of general application which pertain to or affect the operation of this Agreement. International agreements to which a Member is a signatory pertaining to or affecting labor migration shall also be published.

4.2. Where publication as referred to in paragraph 1 is not practicable, such information shall be made publicly available otherwise.

4.3. Each Member shall promptly and at least annually inform the Council for Migration of the introduction of any new, or any changes to existing, laws, regulations, or administrative guidelines which significantly affect migration covered by its specific commitments under this Agreement.

4.4. Each Member shall respond promptly to all requests by any other Member for specific information on any of its measures of general application or international agreements within the meaning of paragraph 1. Each Member shall also establish one or more enquiry points to provide specific information to other Members, upon request, on all such matters as well as those subject to the notification requirement in paragraph 3. Such enquiry points shall be established within one year from the date of entry into force of this Agreement. Appropriate flexibility with respect to the time limit within which such enquiry points are to be established may be agreed upon for individual developing country Members. Enquiry points need not be depositories of laws and regulations.

4.5. Any Member may notify to the Council for Migration any measure, taken by any other Member, which it considers affects the operation of this Agreement.

4.6. Nothing in this Agreement shall require any Member to provide confidential information, the disclosure of which would impede law enforcement, or otherwise be contrary to the public interest, or which would prejudice legitimate commercial interests of particular enterprises, public or private.

5. Labor Market Access Commitments

5.1. Each Member shall set out in a schedule appended to this Agreement the specific commitments it undertakes under this Agreement.

5.1.1. Commitments shall be structured in any of the following ways:

5.1.1.1. *Horizontal Commitments.* Horizontal commitments relate to all immigrants.

5.1.1.2. *Occupational Title Commitments.* Vertical occupational title commitments relate to immigrants who are categorized within a particular occupational title. Wherever possible, each Member shall utilize the International Standard Classification of Occupations 2008, as in force on the date hereof ("ISCO 2008"), as a basis for its occupational title commitments. Each Member shall publish a set of definitions of each occupational title, showing how its definitions differ from the relevant ISCO 2008 definitions.

5.1.1.3. *Occupational Group Commitments.* Vertical occupational group commitments relate to immigrants who are categorized within a particular occupational group. Wherever possible, each Member shall utilize the ISCO 2008, as a basis for its occupational group commitments. Each Member shall publish a set of definitions of each occupational group, showing how its definitions differ from the relevant ISCO 2008 definitions.

5.1.1.4. *Skill Level Commitments.* Skill level commitments relate to immigrants who are categorized within a particular skill level group. Wherever possible, each Member shall utilize the ISCO 2008 skill level group definitions, as a basis for its skill level commitments. Each Member shall publish a set of definitions of each skill level, showing how its definitions differ from the relevant ISCO 2008 definitions.

5.1.1.5. *Wealth Level Commitments.* Wealth level commitments relate to the net worth of the individual immigrant or family of immigrants, and shall be specified in the Schedule of Commitments in terms of a monetary amount, as well as a statement as to evidentiary requirements required to be met in order to qualify under these commitments.

5.1.2. With respect to each commitment undertaken, each Schedule shall specify:

5.1.2.1. distinctions, where desired, between those who already have accepted a job offer in the destination Member, and those who wish to enter the labor market of the destination Member;
5.1.2.2. terms, limitations, and conditions on access;
5.1.2.3. conditions and limitations on national treatment;
5.1.2.4. undertakings relating to additional commitments;
5.1.2.5. where appropriate, the time frame for implementation of such commitments;
5.1.2.6. the date of entry into force of such commitments.

5.1.3. Schedules of specific commitments shall be annexed to this Agreement and shall form an integral part thereof.

5.2. With respect to labor market access, including the issuance of a visa (if necessary) and entry, each Member shall accord citizens of any other Member treatment no less favourable than that provided for under the terms, limitations and conditions agreed and specified in its Schedule.

5.3. Quota for entry. A Member may specify within their schedules as to a specific classification of immigrant such quotas or other numerical limit on entry as such Member shall determine.

5.4. Immigration fee or discriminatory tax. Members may specify within their Schedules as to a specific classification of immigrant, from a specific home Member, that such immigrants shall be subject to an immigration fee, or an income tax that may be greater or less than that ordinarily applicable to citizens or residents. To the extent that the tax is greater than that ordinarily applicable to citizens, the collecting Member shall, as specified in its schedule, either (i) apply the proceeds in a manner reasonably designed to provide adjustment assistance to citizens or residents who have experienced economic dislocation due to immigration, and shall notify the Council for Migration annually of the details of such application, or (ii) transfer the proceeds representing the excess of the applied tax over that ordinarily applicable to citizens to the home Member in respect of the subject immigrant.

5.5. Restrictions on term of residence, if any. A Member may specify within its Schedule as to a specific classification of immigrant such temporal or other limitations on the term of residence of such immigrant as such Member shall determine.

5.6. Entry of family members. A Member may specify within its schedules as to a specific classification of immigrant such provisions relating to permission for entry of family members and national treatment of family members as such Member may determine; provided, however, that any immigrant who resides or is expected to reside in the territory of a Member for a period greater than one year shall be permitted to be accompanied by such immigrant's spouse or domestic partner, children, or parents.

5.7. Members may negotiate commitments with respect to measures affecting immigration, including those regarding qualifications or licensing matters. Such commitments shall be inscribed in a Member's Schedule.

6. Prohibition of other Quantitative or Economic Restrictions, Including Labor Market Certification Arrangements.

   6.1. Other than the types of restrictions permitted to be included in Members' Schedules pursuant to Article 5, Members shall apply no quantitative restrictions on immigrants.

   6.2. "Quantitative restrictions" include not only quotas but also, without limitation, labor market certification requirements, competitive needs tests, minimum wages (other than generally applicable minimum wages applied without discrimination by nationality) or other similar labor market condition-based restrictions or conditions on entry.

7. MFN in Entry

   7.1. With respect to any measure covered by this Agreement, except as specifically provided in this Agreement, each Member shall accord immediately and unconditionally to citizens of any other Member treatment no less favourable than that it accords to like citizens of any other country.

   7.2. Where a Member maintains a quota on immigration, such quota shall be allocated among home countries. The Member applying the restrictions may seek agreement with all other Members having a substantial interest with respect to the allocation of shares in the quota. In cases in which this method is not reasonably practicable, the Member concerned shall allot to Members having a substantial interest shares based upon the proportions of immigrants supplied by such Members during a previous representative period, due account being taken of any special factors which may have affected or may be affecting immigration.

   7.3. A Member may maintain a measure inconsistent with paragraph 1 provided that such a measure is listed in, and meets the conditions of, the Annex on Article 7 Exemptions.

7.4. The provisions of this Agreement shall not be so construed as to prevent any Member from conferring or according advantages to adjacent countries in order to facilitate short-term migration limited to contiguous frontier zones.

8. MFN Exceptions for Existing Arrangements, Including Bilateral Labor Agreements

8.1. This Agreement shall not prevent any of its Members from being a party to or entering into an agreement liberalizing labor migration between or among the parties to such an agreement, provided that such an agreement:

8.1.1. provides for substantial liberalization of immigration restrictions in both high-skilled and low-skilled occupations,
8.1.2. has substantial occupational coverage, and
8.1.3. provides for the absence or elimination of substantially all discrimination, in the sense of Article 11, between or among the parties, in the occupations covered under subparagraphs 1 and 2, through:

8.1.3.1. elimination of existing discriminatory measures, and/or
8.1.3.2. prohibition of new or more discriminatory measures, either at the entry into force of that agreement or on the basis of a reasonable time frame, except for measures permitted under Article 11 and exceptional provisions of this Agreement.

8.2. In evaluating whether the conditions under paragraph 1 are met, consideration may be given to the relationship of the agreement to a wider process of labor integration or trade liberalization among the countries concerned.
8.3. Where developing countries are parties to an agreement of the type referred to in paragraph 1, flexibility shall be provided

regarding the conditions set out in paragraph 1, particularly with reference to subparagraph 3 thereof, in accordance with the level of development of the countries concerned, both overall and in individual occupations.

8.4. Any agreement referred to in paragraph 1 shall be designed to facilitate migration between the parties to the agreement and shall not in respect of any Member outside the agreement raise the overall level of barriers to migration within the respective sectors or subsectors compared to the level applicable prior to such an agreement.

8.5. Members that are parties to any agreement referred to in paragraph 1 shall promptly notify any such agreement and any enlargement or any significant modification of that agreement to the Council for Migration. They shall also make available to the Council such relevant information as may be requested by it. The Council may establish a working party to examine such an agreement or enlargement or modification of that agreement and to report to the Council on its consistency with this Article.

8.6. Members that are parties to any agreement referred to in paragraph 1 which is implemented on the basis of a time frame shall report periodically to the Council for Migration on its implementation. The Council may establish a working party to examine such reports if it deems such a working party necessary.

8.7. Based on the reports of the working parties referred to in subparagraphs 5 and 6, the Council may make recommendations to the parties as it deems appropriate.

9. Prohibition of Restrictions on Emigration.

9.1. Members shall not take any measures to restrict or hinder emigration by their citizens and residents.

9.2. The obligations of Members under paragraph 1 shall be subject to exceptions as appropriate on reasonable grounds of protection of national or international public health, national security, and public policy, provided that these exceptions comply with international human rights law.

10. Emigration Tax.

10.1. Notwithstanding any other provision of this Agreement, and notwithstanding any provision in any tax treaty or other treaty in force between Members, home state Members may continue to tax their citizens after emigration to any destination state Member.

10.2. Any tax imposed pursuant to paragraph 1 shall be limited to an amount calculated as specified in the Schedule of Article 10 Taxes of the relevant Member. The relevant Member may reduce the tax specified on such Schedule at any time.

10.3. Any tax imposed pursuant to paragraph 1 shall give rise to a deduction or to a credit under the tax regime of the destination state Member as and to the extent specified in the Schedule of Commitments of the destination Member.

10.4. The destination state Member shall provide full assistance to the home state Member in connection with the collection and enforcement of any tax imposed under paragraph 1.

11. National Treatment

11.1. In the sectors inscribed in its Schedule, and subject to any conditions or qualifications set out therein or elsewhere in this Agreement, each Member shall accord to citizens of any other Member, in respect of all measures affecting immigration, the right to work after entry, and the conditions of work after entry, treatment no less favourable than that it accords to its own like citizens.[1]

11.2. Notwithstanding paragraph 1 of this Article, the treatment a Member accords to citizens of the other Member may be different from the treatment the Member accords to its persons, provided that:

[1] Specific commitments assumed under this Article shall not be construed to require any Member to compensate for any inherent competitive disadvantages which result from the foreign character of the individual.

11.2.1. the difference in treatment is no greater than that necessary for prudential, fiduciary, health and safety or consumer protection reasons; and

11.2.2. such different treatment is equivalent in effect to the treatment accorded by the Member to its ordinary residents for such reasons.

11.3. The Member proposing or according different treatment under paragraph 2 shall have the burden of establishing that such treatment is consistent with that paragraph.

11.4. No provision of this Article shall be construed as imposing obligations or conferring rights upon either Member with respect to government procurement or subsidies.

11.5. Labor organization. Where membership in a labor organization is available to citizens, Members shall ensure that such labor organization admits immigrants under conditions and circumstances that are no less favorable than those that the labor organization accords to citizens of the Member. Any clause of a collective agreement or individual agreement concerning eligibility for employment, remuneration or other conditions of work shall be null and void insofar as it provides for discrimination against nationals of other Members.

11.6. Military service. No migrant under this Agreement shall be obligated to serve in the military service of the destination state, unless and until such individual becomes a citizen of such destination state.

11.7. Notwithstanding any other provision of this Agreement, no Member shall have any obligation under this Agreement to accord to any person the right to vote in political elections, to admit any person to elective or appointive public office, or to allow any person to enlist in its military, police, or other security services.

12. Public services. In addition to the obligations provided under Article 11.1, Members shall ensure that immigrants have equal access to public services provided to citizens, including public education, pub-

lic health services, public housing, police and fire protection services, social work services, and other public services.

13. Coordination of Social Security. In order to provide freedom of movement for workers and self-employed persons, the Members shall, in the field of social security, secure, as provided for in Annex 13, for workers and self-employed persons and their dependants, in particular:

    13.1. aggregation, for the purpose of acquiring and retaining the right to benefit and of calculating the amount of benefit, of all periods taken into account under the laws of the several countries;
    13.2. payment of benefits to persons resident in the territories of Members.

14. Professional Qualifications, Licensing, and Recognition

    14.1. In sectors where specific commitments are undertaken, each Member shall ensure that all measures of general application affecting immigration and authorization to work are administered in a reasonable, objective and impartial manner.
    14.2. Each Member shall maintain or institute as soon as practicable judicial, arbitral or administrative tribunals or procedures which provide, at the request of an affected person, for the prompt review of, and where justified, appropriate remedies for, administrative decisions affecting migration. Where such procedures are not independent of the agency entrusted with the administrative decision concerned, the Member shall ensure that the procedures in fact provide for an objective and impartial review.
    14.3. The provisions of paragraph 2 shall not be construed to require a Member to institute such tribunals or procedures where this would be inconsistent with its constitutional structure or the nature of its legal system.
    14.4. Where authorization is required for the practice of an occupation on which a specific commitment has been made, the competent authorities of a Member shall, within a reasonable

period of time after the submission of an application considered complete under domestic laws and regulations, inform the applicant of the decision concerning the application. At the request of the applicant, the competent authorities of the Member shall provide, without undue delay, information concerning the status of the application.

14.5. With a view to ensuring that measures relating to qualification requirements and procedures and licensing requirements do not constitute unnecessary barriers to immigration, the Council for Migration shall, through appropriate bodies it may establish, develop any necessary disciplines. Such disciplines shall aim to ensure that such requirements are, inter alia:

14.5.1. based on objective and transparent criteria, such as competence and the ability to practice the occupation;
14.5.2. not more burdensome than necessary to ensure the quality of the practice of the occupation and to achieve other relevant public policy goals;
14.5.3. in the case of licensing procedures, not in themselves a restriction on immigration.

14.6. In sectors in which a Member has undertaken specific commitments, pending the entry into force of disciplines developed in these sectors pursuant to paragraph 5, the Member shall not apply licensing and qualification requirements that nullify or impair such specific commitments in a manner which:

14.6.1. does not comply with the criteria outlined in subparagraphs 14.5.1, 14.5.2 or 14.5.3; and
14.6.2. could not reasonably have been expected of that Member at the time the specific commitments in those sectors were made.

14.7. In determining whether a Member is in conformity with the obligation under paragraph 6, account shall be taken of international standards of relevant international organizations applied by that Member.[2]

14.8. In sectors where specific commitments regarding professional occupations are undertaken, each Member shall provide for adequate procedures to verify the competence of professionals of any other Member.

15. Recognition.

15.1. For the purposes of the fulfillment, in whole or in part, of its standards or criteria for the authorization, licensing or certification of practitioners of specific occupations, and subject to the requirements of paragraph 3, a Member may recognize the education or experience obtained, requirements met, or licenses or certifications granted in a particular country. Such recognition, which may be achieved through harmonization or otherwise, may be based upon an agreement or arrangement with the country concerned or may be accorded autonomously.

15.2. A Member that is a party to an agreement or arrangement of the type referred to in paragraph 1, whether existing or future, shall afford adequate opportunity for other interested Members to negotiate their accession to such an agreement or arrangement or to negotiate comparable ones with it. Where a Member accords recognition autonomously, it shall afford adequate opportunity for any other Member to demonstrate that education, experience, licenses, or certifications obtained or requirements met in that other Member's territory should be recognized.

15.3. A Member shall not accord recognition in a manner which would constitute a means of discrimination between countries in the application of its standards or criteria for the authorization, licensing or certification of practitioners of specific occupations, or a disguised restriction on migration.

[2] The term "relevant international organizations" refers to international bodies whose membership is open to the relevant bodies of at least all Members.

15.4. Each Member shall:

15.4.1. within 12 months from the date on which this Agreement takes effect for it, inform the Council for Migration of its existing recognition measures and state whether such measures are based on agreements or arrangements of the type referred to in paragraph 1;

15.4.2. promptly inform the Council for Migration as far in advance as possible of the opening of negotiations on an agreement or arrangement of the type referred to in paragraph 1 in order to provide adequate opportunity to any other Member to indicate their interest in participating in the negotiations before they enter a substantive phase;

15.4.3. promptly inform the Council for Migration when it adopts new recognition measures or significantly modifies existing ones and state whether the measures are based on an agreement or arrangement of the type referred to in paragraph 1.

16. Permission for Remittances in Host State and Home State. Members shall not prohibit or inhibit the freedom of migrants to transfer funds earned by their work, subject to the observance of applicable law relating to regulation of money laundering, taxation, or judicial orders, or other reasonable regulatory purposes.

17. Economic Safeguards

17.1. In the event of a labor market disturbance that a Member has determined, pursuant to the provisions below, seriously threatens or causes serious injury to that Member's affected citizens' standard of living in a particular labor market of that Member (the "relevant labor market"), that Member may, as a safeguards measure, temporarily derogate from the relevant liberalization commitments specified in its Schedule, to the extent and for such time as may be necessary to prevent or remedy such injury. Under no circumstances shall such temporary exception be applied for longer than six months. Any Member taking such measure shall communicate the circumstance and the period of the exception to the Secretariat, which shall notify the other Members.

17.2. Safeguard measures shall be applied by restricting entry of new immigrants in accordance with the most-favored nation principles of Articles 7 and 8 of this Agreement.

17.3. Safeguard measures shall not be applied in any way to affect the position of immigrants who arrived prior to the determination specified in paragraph 1. Nor shall any form of expulsion be applied in connection with immigrants who immigrate pursuant to this Agreement,

17.4. A Member may apply a safeguard measure only following an investigation by the competent authorities of that Member pursuant to procedures previously established and made public in consonance with Article 4. This investigation shall include reasonable public notice to all interested parties and public hearings or other appropriate means in which employers, workers, and other interested parties may present evidence and their views, including the opportunity to respond to the presentations of other parties and to submit their views, inter alia, as to whether or not the application of a safeguard measure would be in the public interest. The competent authorities shall publish a report setting forth their findings and reasoned conclusions reached on all pertinent issues of fact and law.

17.5. For the purposes of this Agreement:

17.5.1. "serious injury" shall be understood to mean a significant overall impairment in the position of workers in a relevant labor market;

17.5.2. "threat of serious injury" shall be understood to mean serious injury that is clearly imminent. A determination of the existence of a threat of serious injury shall be based on facts and not merely on allegation, conjecture or remote possibility;

17.5.3. in determining injury or threat thereof, a "relevant labor market" shall be understood to mean the workers as a whole who are directly competitive with one another such that the entry into the market of additional workers has a direct and significant effect on the wages of incumbent workers.

17.6. In the investigation to determine whether a labor market disturbance has caused or is threatening to cause serious injury to affected citizens' standard of living in a relevant labor market of a Member under the terms of this Agreement, the competent authorities shall evaluate all relevant factors of an objective and quantifiable nature having a bearing on the situation of that labor market. The determination referred to in subparagraph 1 shall not be made unless this investigation demonstrates, on the basis of objective evidence, the existence of a causal link between a labor market disturbance in the relevant labor market and serious injury or threat thereof. When factors other than the labor market disturbance are causing injury to the relevant labor market at the same time, such injury shall not be attributed to the labor market disturbance. The competent authorities shall publish promptly a detailed analysis of the case under investigation as well as a demonstration of the relevance of the factors examined.

17.7. Any safeguards measure taken under this Article shall be accompanied, within six months, by a program of adjustment assistance undertaken by the Member taking the safeguards measure. Such program of adjustment assistance shall be sufficient to ensure that the significant overall impairment in the position of workers in the relevant labor market is ameliorated.

17.8. A Member shall apply safeguard measures only to the extent necessary to prevent or remedy serious injury and to facilitate adjustment. If a quantitative restriction is used, such a measure shall not reduce the quantity of immigration below the level of a recent period which shall be the average of immigration in the last three representative years for which statistics are available, unless clear justification is given that a different level is necessary to prevent or remedy serious injury. Members should choose measures most suitable for the achievement of these objectives.

17.9. In cases in which a quota is allocated among home countries, the Member applying the restrictions may seek agreement with respect to the allocation of shares in the quota with all other Members having a substantial interest. In cases in which this method is not reasonably practicable, the Member concerned shall allot to Members having a substantial interest shares based upon the proportions of immigrants supplied by such Members during a previous representative period, due account being taken of any special factors which may have affected or may be affecting immigration.

18. Public Policy and Public Security Exceptions

18.1. Subject to the provisions of this Article, Members may derogate from their commitments under this Agreement, on grounds of public policy or public security. These grounds shall not be invoked to serve economic ends.

18.2. Measures taken on grounds of public policy or public security shall comply with the principle of proportionality and shall be based exclusively on the personal conduct of the individual concerned.

18.3. The personal conduct of the individual concerned must represent a genuine, present and sufficiently serious threat affecting one of the fundamental interests of society. Justifications that are isolated from the particulars of the case or that rely on considerations of general prevention shall not be accepted.

18.4. In order to ascertain whether the person concerned represents a danger for public policy or public security, the host Member may, should it consider this essential, request the home Member and, if need be, other Members, to provide information concerning any previous police record the person concerned may have. Such enquiries shall not be made as a matter of routine. The Member consulted shall give its reply within two months.

19. Public Health Exceptions

    19.1. Members retain the right to take action in order to protect national and international public health, pursuant to the provisions of this Article.
    19.2. The only diseases justifying derogations from the commitments undertaken pursuant to this Agreement shall be the diseases with epidemic potential as defined by the relevant instruments of the World Health Organization and other infectious diseases or contagious parasitic diseases if they are the subject of protection provisions applying to nationals of the host Member.
    19.3. Diseases occurring after a three-month period from the date of arrival shall not constitute grounds for expulsion from the territory of the host Member.
    19.4. Where there are serious indications that it is necessary, Members may, within three months of the date of arrival, require immigrants to undergo, free of charge, a medical examination to certify that they are not suffering from any of the conditions referred to in paragraph 2. Such medical examinations may not be required as a matter of routine.

20. Right of Return. The home Member of any person who has left any destination state for any reason, including without limitation if such person has been expelled on grounds of public policy, public security, or public health, shall allow that person to return at any time from another Member and to re-enter its territory without any formality even if the nationality of the holder is in dispute.
21. Protection Against Expulsion

    21.1. Before taking an expulsion decision on grounds of public policy or public security, the host Member shall take account of considerations such as how long the individual concerned has resided on its territory, his/her age, state of health, family and economic situation, social and cultural integration into the host Member and the extent of his/her links with the country of origin.

21.2. The host Member may not take an expulsion decision against persons who have the right of permanent residence on its territory, except on serious grounds of public policy or public security.

21.3. An expulsion decision may not be taken except if the decision is based on imperative grounds of public security, as defined by Member, if they:

21.3.1. have resided in the host Member for the previous 10 years; or

21.3.2. are a minor, except if the expulsion is necessary for the best interests of the child, as provided for in the United Nations Convention on the Rights of the Child of 20 November 1989.

22. Cooperation in Reduction of Unauthorized Migration. Members shall exercise their best efforts to cooperate with other Members in discouraging and preventing unauthorized migration.

23. Progressive Liberalization.

23.1. In pursuance of the objectives of this Agreement, Members shall enter into successive rounds of negotiations, beginning not later than five years from the date of entry into force of this Agreement and periodically thereafter, with a view to achieving a progressively higher level of liberalization. Such negotiations shall be directed to the reduction or elimination of barriers to migration. This process shall take place with a view to promoting the interests of all participants on a mutually advantageous basis and to securing an overall balance of rights and obligations.

23.2. The process of liberalization shall take place with due respect for national policy objectives and the level of development of individual Members, both overall and in individual sectors. There shall be appropriate flexibility for individual developing country Members for liberalization in line with their development situation and, when making access to their markets available to foreign persons, attaching to such access conditions aimed at achieving their development objectives.

23.3. For each round, negotiating guidelines and procedures shall be established. For the purposes of establishing such guidelines, the Secretariat shall carry out an assessment of migration in overall terms and on a sectoral basis with reference to the objectives of this Agreement, including its development objectives.

23.4. The process of progressive liberalization shall be advanced in each such round through bilateral, plurilateral, or multilateral negotiations directed toward increasing the general level of specific commitments undertaken by Members under this Agreement.

24. Loyalty. Member governments shall refrain from disparaging the labor market, cultural, political or ethnic effects or contributions of immigrants. Member governments shall ensure that any official analyses of labor market conditions follow sound social scientific methods of establishing causal relationships.

25. Relationship to International Human Rights and Labor Rights Treaties.

25.1. Except as specifically provided in their Schedules, Members shall comply with the Migration for Employment Convention of 1949 (No. 97), including Optional Annex 1 thereof, the Migrant Workers (Supplementary Provisions) Convention of 1975 (No. 143) and the International Convention on the Protection of the Rights of All Migrant Workers and Their Families.

25.2. With respect to migrants, Members shall comply with the International Covenant on Civil and Political Rights.

25.3. [other human rights and labor rights instruments to be listed]

26. Relationship to Other Treaties
    26.1. Relationship to International Tax Treaties
    26.2. Relationship to International Investment Treaties
    26.3. Relationship to International Trade Treaties
27. Secretariat and Funding
28. Decision-Making
29. Dispute Settlement
30. Final Provisions

References

Agarwal A., D. Kapur, and J. McHale. 2008. Brain Drain or Brain Bank? The Impact of Skilled Emigration on Poor-country Innovation. NBER Working Paper 1459w2Mooe *2008,* Brian Drain or Bran Bank.

Aleinikoff, T.A. 2016. The UN refugee summit: What can be achieved? ag.

Bergsten, C.F. 1994. Managing the world economy of the future. In *Managing the world economy*, ed. Peter B. Kenen. Washington, DC: Institute for International Economics.

Bonnin, H., et al. 2000. Can immigration alleviate the demographic burden? *FinanzArchiv: Public Finance Analysis* 57 (1): 1–21.

Clemens, M.A. 2011. Economics and emigration: Trillion-dollar bills on the sidewalk. *Journal of Economic Perspectives* 25 (3): 83–106.

Coggio, T. 2021. "Europe's Tackling of Root Causes of African Migration had a Mixed Record". Source: Migration Information Source, MPI, Washington DC. 6 May 2021.

Commission on Global Governance. 1995. *Our global neighbourhood: The report of the commission on global governance*. Oxford University Press.

Contini, B. 1982. The second economy. In *The underground economy in the United States and abroad*, ed. V. Tanzi.

Eichengreen, B., and P. Kenen. 1994. Managing the world economy under the Bretton woods system: An overview. In *Managing the world economy*, ed. Peter Kenen, 54. Washington, DC: Institute for International Economics.

B. Ghosh, *The 2018 Global Migration Compact*,
https://doi.org/10.1007/978-3-030-82863-9

EUROSTAT, European Commission. "Demographics of the European Union", Luxembourg 2002.

European Commission. 1998.

——— (2116) Press Release 6 June 2016. Partnership framework for a coordinated, systematic and structural approach matching the EU's interests with the interests of our partners.

Financial Times, London, 28 May 2002.

G-20 Leaders Communique Antalya Summit. 15–16 November 2015. http://europeansting.com/2015/11/16/g20live-g20-live

Ghosh, B. 1997. Labour migration: Causes, conditions and consequences. key note paper presented at the world congress on globalisation, migration and the labour market, Nuremberg, May 1997.

———. 1998a. Tame Europe's black economy in *International Herald Tribune*, 10 June 1998.

———. 1998b. *Huddled masses and uncertain shores: Insight into irregular migration*. The Hague: Martinus Nijhoff Publishers/Kluwer Law International.

———. 2000a. *Managing migration: Time for a new international regime?* Oxford, UK: Oxford University Press.

———. 2000b. *Return migration: A journey of hope or despair.*

———. 2003. *Elusive protection, uncertain lands: Migrants' access to human rights*. Geneva: IOM.

———. 2005a. Economic effects of international migration: A synoptic overview. In *World migration report, 2005, costs and benefits of international migration*. IOM.

———. 2005b. The challenge of integration: A global perspective. In *Managing integration*, ed. Rita Sussmuth and Werner Weidenfeld.

———. 2005c. Managing migration: Interstate cooperation at the global level: Is the emergence of a new paradigm of partnership around the corner?

———. 2007. *Managing migration: Towards the missing regime*,

———. 2008. *Human rights and migration: The missing link*. Utrecht: University of Utrecht.

Goodwin-Gill, Guy S. 2000. Migration: International law and human rights. In *Managing migration: Time for a new international regime?* ed. Bimal Ghosh. Oxford: Oxford University Press.

Hamilton, B., and J. Whalley. 1984. Efficiency and distributional implications of global restrictions on labour mobility. *Journal of Development Economics* 1414: 61–75.

ILO. International Labour Conference, *Migrant Workers*. Geneva 1999.

International Chamber of Commerce, Barriers to International Travel; *Report of its committee of experts for the simplification of formalities in international transport.* February 1947. Brochure no. 105.

Jaumotte, Florence et al. 2016. Impact of migration on income levels in advanced economies. IMF e Library, October 2016.

Krogstad, Passel and Cohen, 2017. Migration Data Portal 9 June 2020.

Kovacheva and Vogel, 2009. Migration Data Portal 9 June 2020.

Meissner, D.M., et al. 1993. *International migration challenges in a new era.* New York: Trilateral Commission.

Migrant Files. 2015. http://www.themigrantfiles.com

Moses, Jonathan, et al. 2004. The economic costs to international labour restrictions: Revisiting the empirical discussion. In *World development.* World Bank.

OECD "Is Migration Good for the Economy" Migration Policy Debate 2014. Paris.

Ogata, S. 1992. *Refugees: A multilateral response to humanitarian crises.* Berkley: Institute of International Studies, University of California. April, 1992.

Purcell, J.N. Jr. 1993. The world needs a policy for orderly migration. *International Herald Tribune*, 8 July 1993.

Rodrik, D. 2002. Feasible globalizations. In *Globalization: What's new?* ed. M. Weinstein, 96–213. New York: Colombia University Press. Also, working paper series RWP02029, pp.19–20.

Straubhaar, T. 1994. Migration pressures. *International Migration* 31: 15–41.

UNFPA, Executive Summary. 1998. *Technical symposium on international migration and development*, 34. The Hague, June–July 1998.

Weiss, L. 1987. Explaining the underground economy: State and social structure. *British Journal of Sociology* 38.

World Bank: "Gains from Migration" 2005. Washington DC.

Lightning Source UK Ltd.
Milton Keynes UK
UKHW011946091221
395409UK00002B/79